Siân Evans

# Life below Stairs

### In the Victorian & Edwardian Country House

Siân Evans

# Life below Stairs

In the Victorian
& Edwardian
Country House

National Trust

*For my parents, Rae and David*

First published in Great Britain in 2011 by National Trust Books

This edition first published in Great Britain in 2015 by
National Trust Books
1 Gower Street
London WC1E 6HD
An imprint of Pavilion Books Company Ltd

ISBN: 9781909881648

A CIP catalogue record for this book is available from
the British Library.

20 19 18 17 16 15
10 9 8 7 6 5 4 3 2 1

Reproduction by Mission Productions Ltd, Hong Kong
Printed and bound by 1010 Printing International Ltd, China

This book can be ordered direct from the publisher at the website:
www.pavilionbooks.com, or try your local bookshop. Also available at
National Trust shops, including www.nationaltrustbooks.co.uk.

# Contents

Page 2: The fireplace in the Housekeeper's Room at Uppark, Sussex.

Left: Servants' bells in the corridor next to the Stillroom at Dunham Massey, Cheshire.

# INTRODUCTION

No matter what our individual backgrounds, all our forebears either worked for other people, or had other people working for them. Statistically, our ancestors are more likely to have fetched and carried, cooked and cleaned for others, than to have issued instructions to servants.

In previous centuries in Britain, vast armies of people spent their working lives in domestic service: between 1700 and 1900, nearly 15 per cent of the working population were domestic servants. Some were dedicated and reliable, trusted members of the household. Others saw 'service' as an opportunity to better themselves and acquire a useful trade in the homes of the wealthy. The majority of servants' personal histories went largely unrecorded; before the advent of universal education in the 1870s, people from humble backgrounds would only have a rough working knowledge of their 'letters' and numbers. They were kept occupied all day, with almost no free time, and had few opportunities to write detailed accounts of their lives.

However clues on paper survive. There are cellar books written by butlers, often in an increasingly spidery scrawl; house stewards' records of wages paid, staff dismissed or replaced; blotted missives with idiosyncratic spelling from the housekeeper to inform the mistress that there are moths in the hangings, and terse four-fold notes to butlers from their masters, commanding urgent preparations for a royal visit. Down in the basement, a home remedy for gout has been laboriously transcribed into the cook's battered 'book of receipts'.

Written and recorded accounts portray the everyday life in a great house. Those 'upstairs' recall the sumptuous tea trays, the sparkling silver, the galaxy of candles lit and extinguished, night after night. The denizens of 'downstairs'

Below: A group portrait of staff on the garden steps at Erddig in the early twentieth century. With cook at the centre and the male staff on the top step, photographs of servants from this era reveal the social pyramid of life 'below stairs'.

have more prosaic memories: the great hillocks of coal fed into the insatiable kitchen range, the heat, the steam, the smell of old cabbage and yellow soap, the black beetles, the misshapen shoes and worn corsets, the 'plate' hands and the aching backs. Above all, they recall the need for absolute silence and invisibility once on the other side of the green baize door.

*O let us love our occupations,*
*Bless the squire and his relations,*
*Live upon our daily rations,*
*And always know our proper stations.*

Charles Dickens, 'The Chimes', 1844

There are forensic clues, too, in old houses: the uneven flagstones, worn by the footfall of boots; the texture of the enormous, ancient kitchen table, sanded down and scalded with hot water every morning for hundreds of years, leaving the grain exposed like the ridges of a beach at low tide; the metal fatigue in the wires that connect the bell-pull in the drawing room to the bellboard in the servants' corridor.

This book examines the secret lives of servants, those who worked to sustain the aspirational lifestyles of the wealthy in the nineteenth and early twentieth centuries. The majority of these lives went unrecorded at the time, and the people who lived them are now largely forgotten. But, if we know where to look, there is a vast archive of material, from oral testimonies to handwritten notebooks, anarchic graffiti to printed 'Rules for Servants' still hanging in servants' halls, which can tell us much about the texture of everyday 'life below stairs'.

Above: The Kitchen at Canons Ashby, with Victorian cast-iron range and cooking utensils and stone flagged floor. The row of bells governed all aspects of servants' lives.

# *1* LIFE IN SERVICE

The idea that being a servant is somehow degrading or demeaning is comparatively recent. In the Middle Ages, society was feudal. Landowners had considerable power over 'their' peasants, whose lives were dangerous, dirty and dependent upon the whims of their lord and the success of the next harvest. Joining an aristocrat's household was an opportunity for social advancement. As a member of a noble 'family', a servant would be physically protected, have a better standard of living and gain higher social status.

There were three main routes to advancement: the Church, the Law or seeking a post in a great household. For the less spiritual or cerebral, service was an attractive option. Within each noble household, a hierarchy existed; the 'officer classes' were often of higher birth and they acted as stewards or ushers, running the household and controlling the yeomen servants. In Britain, the nobility placed their offspring in other aristocratic households, once they were eight or nine years old, so that they could be taught social skills, manners and decorum. This system of 'farming out' children to forge useful alliances and glean an education under another's roof eventually evolved to become the English public-school system.

Every occupant of a great house owed a debt of loyalty and fealty to their lord. The medieval lord and master referred to his household as his 'family'; landowners still sometimes refer to 'our people' when talking of their tenants and staff. Medieval women servants worked as ladies' maids, laundresses or nursemaids; all other duties, such as those of the cook, were performed by men. Partly this was an inevitable consequence of living in dangerous times: menservants doubled as bodyguards or soldiers, to repel raiding parties or to defend the household's wealth.

At its peak, an important estate such as Knole in Kent required a huge army of servants, encompassing many trades and occupations. Maintaining a large household remained a status symbol throughout the Tudor era.

*Great state was observed here once, when well over a hundred servants sat down daily to eat at long tables in the Great Hall... all coming in from their bothies and outhouses to share in the communal meal with their master, his lady, their children, their guests, and the mob of indoor servants whose avocations ranged from His Lordship's Favourite through innumerable pages, attendants, grooms and yeomen of various chambers, scriveners, pantry men, maids, clerks of the kitchen and the buttery...*

Vita Sackville-West, *Knole and the Sackvilles*, 1922

The numbers of women in service began to grow; inevitably, they were paid less than the menservants. By the 1730s, landowners recruited locally from their tenant farmers and estate workers, and existing servants' families. Tenants' children had a well-developed sense of deference and an understanding of what service involved. They could be trained by their parents or siblings, who were already working in the 'Big House'. In this way successive generations of landowning families came to be served by the children and grandchildren of locally born servants. A mutual reliance was established between the landowner's family and the local retainers.

Below: *Bird's Eye View of Knole from the South* (c.1705) by Jan Kip at Knole in Kent. Many workers were needed to run such a large estate, both inside and out.

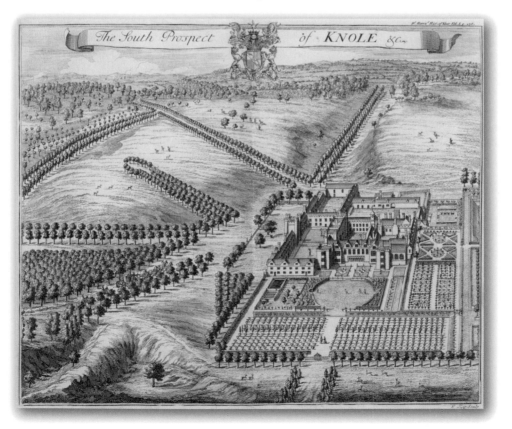

Above: The butler inspects the new housemaid, warning her that her progress is in his hands (1906). The social hierarchy was as strong below stairs as it was above.

# A better life?

In rural districts poverty was rife. Cottages were often small and badly maintained, with water drawn from a well or communal pump. Money was tight and food was scarce, particularly during the agricultural depressions of the 1840s and 1880s. In addition, labouring families had many children who needed feeding and clothing. The chance to place a son or daughter in service in the local 'Big House' was attractive; the child would bring in a small salary to ease stretched finances and be housed, clothed and fed.

The rookie servant needed to be more than ten years old and have attained education certificates for Standard V in reading, writing and arithmetic. Before the 1870s, a basic knowledge of reading and writing was usually provided by the village school, often run as a charity. Philanthropic families were often keen to take on disadvantaged young people; the Robartes family of Lanhydrock employed children from the nearby orphanage and from the workhouses of south London.

Experienced female servants usually left service on marriage, but if their circumstances changed, they were often welcomed back; widows who had been head parlourmaids, for example, might return to a familiar household as housekeeper. Recruiting servants was an ordeal for mistresses: Jane Carlyle recounted an interview at her house in Cheyne Row, Chelsea, where she was subjected to sustained questioning by an aggressive applicant 'with a face to split a pitcher'. Between 1849 and 1853, she employed ten unsatisfactory maids, one leaving after only a fortnight, complaining that it was impossible for anyone to manage the workload expected of her. The Carlyles tended to recruit servants from their native Scotland, but this was not always successful; one, from Kirkcaldy, took to the bottle and had to be dismissed, a painful process for all involved.

Neither was every servant happy in their early years in service; fitting into a complex organisation, with its own inexplicable rules, was never simple. Osbert Sitwell's cook-housekeeper, the redoubtable Mrs Powell, went into service in the late nineteenth century at the age of 13. Sitwell commented, in his book *Laughter in the Next Room* (1950), on Mrs Powell's 'resentment at having been sold into slavery… she had been still a child, and had suffered acutely from homesickness, crying herself to sleep every night in an attic at Castle Howard, above the cupids and allegorical figures, and under the beams of the great house in which she had been given her first situation. All her money had to be sent to her parents…'

# Upstairs and downstairs

Until the eighteenth century, servants often slept in the same rooms as their employers, tucked up on a smaller bed that could be stored during daylight hours, so as to be close at hand. They also 'waited' upon their superiors, constantly within earshot if not actually in the same room. The physical proximity of master and servant began to change with new notions of privacy.

It had been hard to keep any personal secrets from other members of the household – every quarrel or sniffle was likely to be overheard. The creation of separate servants' quarters, from which a servant could be summoned by a bell, changed forever the relationship between employer and employee. Servants and their less palatable tasks became invisible – by providing discreet backstairs for the exclusive use of staff, householders could avoid encountering their servants on the main staircase carrying their chamber pots.

As the family withdrew to their own private rooms, so the servants were 'demoted' in their own eyes to their own quarters, often below ground. The servants' hall at Ham House in Richmond was in the basement, and the sleeping quarters were in the attics, accessible by a narrow staircase installed specifically to separate the domestics from the family. Servants' accommodation was situated at the furthest outposts of the house. Bedrooms or dormitories were under the eaves for female staff and in the basement or over the stables for the men. At both Petworth House and Uppark in Sussex, kitchens were erected to be independent from the main building, and hidden from it. Adjacent service areas were built to encompass storage rooms and larders, sculleries and bake houses, dairies and cold rooms, brushing and lamp rooms.

In the nineteenth century, rooms that had previously been multipurpose, even in the grandest houses, came to be more rigorously defined, with the superior spaces occupied by the householder and his family. At Lanhydrock in Cornwall, it is very evident where the border lies between the 'front of house' and 'backstage' areas – the strong contrast in materials and finishes distinguishes the working world from the leisured one. There were further distinctions 'upstairs': certain rooms were deemed suitable

for receiving and entertaining guests, while others were for the use of family members and their trusted servants only.

The landowning classes were changing. Those who had made their money recently through industry and in cities viewed the acquisition of a country estate as irresistible. Bespoke estates such as Tyntesfield near Bristol and Cragside in Northumberland were built by businessmen and inventors. Of course, even 'old money' was 'new money' originally, but this era of British history is rife with grandiose ambitions fulfilled by gifted inventors and resolute entrepreneurs. Sir William Armstrong, inventor and arms manufacturer, commissioned the best architect of the day to create the country house and estate of Cragside, a technological marvel that would be the envy of all who saw it. Julius Drewe, the founder of the Home and Colonial Stores, was so wealthy that he was able to retire before he was 40 and devote the remainder of his life to creating the redoubtable fortress that his distant forebears would have left to him, if only they had indeed been aristocrats. Castle Drogo in Devon fulfilled a desire in its owner to acquire a remote and noble ancestry – even if he had to pay handsomely to do so.

Status was different from class; the new plutocracy were able to buy their way into society through association with the Prince of Wales, the future Edward VII. 'Tum-tum', as he was known (though never to his face), enjoyed the company of wealthy, worldly men and beautiful, compliant women. Shooting, yachting, visiting country

Above: The Kitchen at Lindisfarne, designed by Lutyens in the early twentieth century. Lutyens wrote eloquently about kitchens and designed them to be efficient and attractive workplaces.

houses and racing were among his favourite diversions, much disapproved of by his perpetually mourning mother, Queen Victoria. His friends and acolytes, known as the Marlborough House Set, acquired or built magnificent country houses where they could surround themselves with every luxury and attract eminent guests. Expanding railways and improved road systems encouraged greater mobility for all classes, and country-house visiting became more practical. Entertaining one's social equals meant maintaining a large and complex household, complete with accomplished, professional and discreet servants. In addition, guests would often bring their own servants, who also needed to be housed, fed and watered.

By the end of the nineteenth century the great country houses of England were the nexus of power, where political deals were cut and alliances made during sociable, hedonistic weekends. Ironically, in many cases only the independently wealthy could afford to run enormous estates. Between 1875 and 1897 cheap food imports from abroad caused rural rents to plummet and the value of agricultural land accordingly fell from £54 to £19 an acre. New landowners used cash from the real source of their wealth, whether it was manufacturing, coal, shipping, retail or banking, to subsidise their country estates. Aristocratic families dependent on the rents and revenues from their estates suffered. Between 1870 and 1919, some 79 major country estates were liquidated or sold in England, Wales and Scotland.

The newly rich often saw their servants primarily as employees, sometimes truculent and uncooperative ones. Deference, discretion, honesty and an ability to merge into the background were the qualities favoured in a servant. In return, the domestics wanted job security, physical comfort and the benign companionship to be found 'below stairs'. They also hoped for a manageable workload rewarded with a fair wage, and the occasional expression of appreciation.

By the middle years of the nineteenth century, one in three females aged between 15 and 20 was working in domestic service. According to the 1871 census, there were 1.19 million servants, of whom some 93,000 were cooks and 75,000 were nursemaids. By 1891, the year of peak employment for the servant classes, the total employed in this way numbered 1,549,502. The numbers of staff in grand houses proliferated during the nineteenth century and reached unprecedented heights in the last two or three decades.

# Summoned by bells

Until the eighteenth century, it was usual for servants to 'wait' on their employers – literally, to stand in attendance, ready to receive instructions. In the country house, this practice echoed the traditions in royal or ducal households; but the loss of privacy was the inevitable price paid for the luxury of having a servant at one's beck and call, day and night.

Below: Internal telephone systems – such as this one in the Butler's Pantry at Castle Drogo – created privacy for those both upstairs and downstairs.

The innovative neoclassical architect Robert Adam was employed by the Child family to refashion and redecorate Osterley Park. He improved access for the householders and staff alike, with bedrooms leading off grand corridors, and created service staircases and servants' shortcuts so that the staff could travel discreetly behind the scenes. Adam also introduced the single pulley doorbell, a deceptively simple device. By pulling the knob attached to a robust wire, a person could ring a far-flung bell. Adam installed a network of bells, which allowed the family to summon specific staff from their quarters downstairs whenever required.

Bells, of course, were not a novelty. In 1663 Samuel Pepys mentions ringing a bell hanging outside his bedroom door to summon the

housemaid, and handbells were used by the genteel and the bedridden to request help. However the long-distance bellboard obliterated at a stroke the centuries-old practice of servants 'waiting' in attendance. The new system was not welcomed by domestics; in former times they spent their days observing the family, listening to gossip, enjoying the comfort, warmth, daylight and luxurious amenities of some of the best rooms in the house. Now they were banished to their own communal quarters, far less salubrious, and summoned as required. A ringing bell in the downstairs corridor or servants' hall called the maid or manservant to its source, and the servant would inevitably have to retrace their steps to carry out the command.

The installation of servants' bells was usually undertaken by plumbers or chimney sweeps, who ran the wires along tubes or pipes. The bellboard was usually located in the servants' hall or on the central corridor of the servants' wing. Each bell was labelled, and they varied in size so that, with practice, the servant could tell by the tone which room was 'ringing'. The larger the house, the more complex the bellboard; at Lanhydrock, the electrical bellboard in the kitchen corridor has 24 separate bells, summoning staff to the prayer room or estate office, the nursery or dining room.

## Speaking tubes to telephones

As early as the 1840s, some houses invested in 'speaking tubes', an idea which originated on steamboats. The system saved time and effort on the part of servants, especially in tall, narrow townhouses with many flights of stairs. An airbell or whistle alerted the servants to an 'incoming call'. However, unless the tube was fitted with a cover or bung, it was possible to overhear conversation from one room in the other. Needless to say, these systems were popular with servants, but discarded by their masters once technology provided a more discreet option in the late 1880s, namely the telephone.

A number of grand houses had sophisticated internal phone systems long before they were connected to an external line. At Dunham Massey in the Oak Bedroom there were two telephones, one connected to the butler's pantry to summon food or drink, and the other to call a maid for hot water or to attend to the fire. Cragside had an early telephone system linking one room with another. Technology had made domestic communications swifter and more efficient, but had also inevitably created a palpable barrier between employer and servant.

# 2 THE CHARACTERS BELOW STAIRS

## The household hierarchy

The people living and working in a prominent Victorian household could be represented by a series of concentric circles. At the centre was the family: the landed parents, a nursery full of children, certainly a male 'heir and a spare' to whom the property would pass in time. An assortment of relatives would come to stay for lengthy periods, and some might possibly live on site.

The family's guests and social equals enjoyed similar status; on occasion the household might be privileged to have a royal visit, an honour for all. Grouped closely around the family were the senior and most intimate servants: the house steward or butler (larger households had both), the lady's maid, the valet, the housekeeper and the nanny. The cook or chef usually fell into this category too, though the specialist nature of their jobs distanced them from the privileged intimacy enjoyed by the very closest servants.

Left: Servants at Erddig, Wrexham, photographed in 1912.

The outer circle, on whom the family relied for their expertise and to whom they entrusted their health and welfare, included the coachman or chauffeur, the footmen and the gamekeeper. Then there were the 'footsoldiers', who performed the hard physical toil required to maintain a vast house, clean its contents, and feed its scores of inhabitants. The stillroom maids and the hall boys, the scullery maid, tweeny and junior kitchen maids, the housemaids, laundry maids and the 'odd man', were unlikely ever to be addressed by their employers:

*We were not allowed to speak directly with Lady Penrhyn, who dealt only through the housekeeper or cook. Cook used to go to her room every morning after prayers to discuss the day's meals and get her orders. We never really knew how the gentry lived, and so were quite content.*

Annie Evans, scullery maid at Penrhyn Castle, Gwynedd, 1908

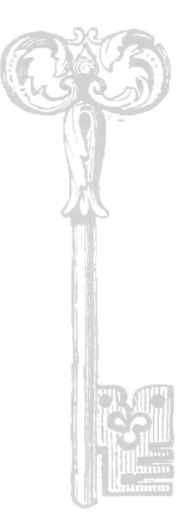

Servants preferred to work for better-connected families because they were treated by staff in other households according to their employer's social status. 'Indoors' staff also thought of themselves as superior to the 'outside' staff; each establishment was like a small court, where proximity to the monarch was a privilege.

There were two distinct ranks of servants within large households. The 'Upper Ten' included the house steward or butler, the housekeeper, the chef or cook, the valet and the lady's maid. The butler's and housekeeper's roles were crucial – they kept the household running smoothly, managing and advising, and hiring and firing staff. As trusted servants, they had a degree of personal contact with the family. In addition, they often took their meals together in the steward's or housekeeper's room, where they were waited on by junior servants. The 'Lower Five', by contrast, formed the numerical majority of household staff and they were expected to avoid undue attention. These less-important figures included the under-butler, the footmen, young-ladies' maids (who assisted the family's juvenile daughters), housemaids, stillroom-, scullery-, kitchen-, laundry- and dairy-maids, coachman, groom, lamp-man or candle-man, 'odd man', steward's room man and servants' hall boy.

The servants' hall was the fulcrum of life 'below stairs'. Even here there were strict hierarchies, and certain privileges were jealously guarded, such as the right to eat in the housekeeper's room. So refined were these distinctions that some staff were employed solely to wait on the upper servants, with no contact with 'upstairs'.

# The house steward

The house steward was a survival from medieval and Tudor times, and typically the master's closest and most trusted assistant. The steward ran the household, looking after the master's business and defending his interests, as well as organising his domestic arrangements.

His duties included hiring, firing and organising the staff, ordering food and supplies, keeping the books and undertaking sensitive duties on behalf of his employer. He took care of the valuables and organised the movement of people and possessions whenever the household moved, perhaps to London for the Season, or to countryside estates for hunting and shooting. The house steward was expected to be a model of discretion and probity, able to mingle at all levels of society and to represent the dignity of his master. In time, the steward's role merged with that of the butler; most households saw no need to maintain two well-paid senior menservants, and the post gradually became defunct.

## The steward's room

In very large houses, upper servants ate in the steward's room, with lower servants eating in the servants' hall. A 'steward's room lad' was usually employed to wait at table on the senior servants, an early training for a future career as a footman.

A typical steward's room was usually located not far from the kitchen but in a separate complex in case of fire. There was a stout external door nearby, so that visitors from outdoors did not need to tramp across the house in muddy boots to reach their destination. Beyond the steward's room was the deeds room, where important legal documents, maps, papers and account books were kept, often in a fireproof safe.

Left: Portrait photograph of William Pattinson, House Steward at Petworth in the 1880s.

## Top house stewards

In the West Country, the title 'steward' often encompassed the duties of a land agent. Silvanus Jenkin was the steward at Lanhydrock, and members of his family served the Robartes family for more than a century. Jenkin was in charge of the butler, the head gardener and the output from the home farm; unusually, he bridged the gap between the indoor staff and the estate staff, and he effectively ran the whole establishment, paying the provisions and wages bills. He commanded the highest wages, between £100 and £125 a year (by comparison, each housemaid at Lanhydrock earned £12 a year). The steward was usually paid about the same amount as a male French chef. At Petworth House the house steward between 1881 and 1899 was Mr Pattinson, who earned £120 a year, the approximate equivalent of £7,186 today. Mr Pattinson dressed as a gentleman, rather than a servant. His accounts detail purchases as diverse as theatre tickets, ginger beer for a cricket match and insecticide. He settled bills from the fishmonger and the greengrocer, and ordered in piano tuners, chimney sweeps and decorators. Many supplies came by mail order, from the department store Harvey Nichols and the tea suppliers Twinings, while HM Prison Portsmouth supplied the household with mops.

# The butler

The word 'butler' derives from the old French noun *bouteiller*, meaning the man in charge of the butts of wine in a medieval household. A peculiarly English invention, the butler was the chief manservant in establishments in which there was no house steward. He organised the male servants, was the link between the master and his staff, and was the repository of many secrets. Lower servants referred to him deferentially as 'Mister', while the family called him by his surname. He worked closely with the housekeeper and cook to ensure the smooth running of all aspects of the house.

Butlers were expected to be bachelors so that they could commit all their time and energy to 'their' family; if a butler claimed to be single and was subsequently found to be maintaining a wife and children, he was usually summarily dismissed. However, the position was well paid; there were tips from visitors and household guests, and expressions of appreciation from vintners and other tradespeople. Occasionally a butler would marry a competent cook or housekeeper in middle age, both of them to go into 'trade' (perhaps running a rather genteel shop) or opening a boarding house or hotel. Claridge's Hotel started as a very superior pied-à-terre in London for good families; Mr and Mrs Claridge had been respectively the butler and housekeeper at a smart address before their marriage.

## The link between upstairs and downstairs

The butler was the most important link between 'upstairs' and 'downstairs', and discretion was vital. He was constantly available, in case any service should be required, but he often managed some time off during the working day, which started at 8am and ended around midnight. He was responsible for ensuring the smooth arrival and departure of guests, for organising where they would sleep, who would look after them and what they would drink. In particular, he had to ensure that every aspect of the table – silver, glass, china and flowers – was perfect.

Butlers were usually promoted from the post of footman, and

*…butlers who weighed two hundred and fifty pounds on the hoof, butlers with three chins and bulging abdomens, butlers with large gooseberry eyes and that austere butlerine manner which has passed so completely away…*

P.G. Wodehouse, *Ring For Jeeves*, 1953

directed the assistance of footmen in their turn. In the Victorian era the butler officiated at breakfast, though by the early twentieth century breakfast had evolved into the labour-saving buffet, with diners helping themselves to the hot and cold dishes lavishly laid out on the sideboard.

The butler might iron the newspapers so as to remove any trace of newsprint, or whiff of ink. He polished the plate, checked on the provision of wine, sherry and port for that evening's dinner, and assisted at luncheon. In the afternoon, the butler was the 'gatekeeper' to the family if they were at home. Visitors arriving at the front door were instantly appraised and categorised as 'gentlefolk' or 'persons'. Gentlefolk were shown straight into the drawing room and announced with due honour. By contrast, 'persons' were those of lower rank, whatever their business. 'A person wishes to see you, Ma'am' was an announcement given all necessary resonance, while the visitor waited anxiously in the hall. The butler would also intone blandly that his mistress was 'not at home' if instructed so to do. This catch-all euphemism was never expanded upon for reasons of discretion, though one contributor to the resolutely Christian *Servants' Magazine* expressed moral concern about the sinfulness of telling a lie, even at the instructions of one's employer.

Below: The butler and footmen at Polesden Lacey in Surrey.

Truth was an elastic concept to many butlers, who often allowed themselves some latitude on afternoons when their employers were out paying calls. Having dispatched the mistress in her carriage, the urban butler would disappear about his own business. Butlers working in rural locations were more inclined to spend the afternoon closeted in their sitting rooms or pantries. This room functioned as an office and a workroom, usually containing a desk or a table where the butler could write and store his timetables and menus, maintain his cellar records, and plan placements for the guest lists for forthcoming events by referring to last year's copy of *Burke's Peerage*, an invaluable guide to finely nuanced social distinctions.

## Dinner duties

Dinner was the highlight of the butler's working day. If guests were expected, the dining table had an extra leaf or two inserted, and then it was elaborately laid by the footmen with freshly ironed napery, under the judicious scrutiny of the butler. The silver was liberated from the plate room or the safe, and carefully inspected for any blemish. Red wine was decanted to give it time to 'breathe' and speculatively tasted to make sure it was palatable and suitable; bottles of white wine and champagne would spend the afternoon in buckets in the cellar, packed in ice to ensure they were suitably cooled. Handwritten menu cards were placed at each setting, so that guests could pace themselves through an obstacle race of courses. The footmen, in full livery, showed their clean hands and well-buffed nails to the butler – nothing escaped his attention.

Below: A wooden sink with lead surround, used for washing fragile and precious items, in the Butler's Pantry at Tyntesfield, Somerset.

Guests arriving for dinner would be welcomed and have their outer garments removed in the hall, before being announced at the door to the drawing room. The butler would dispense aperitifs for 30 minutes or so, then, on receiving a discreet signal conveyed from the kitchen by one of the footmen, he would catch the eye of his hostess and announce 'Dinner is served, ma'am'.

Once the party was seated, and the lesser servants were distributing food, the butler's role was to supervise the wines, help to serve successive courses and to turn a basilisk eye on any lesser servant who transgressed. If the family were dining without guests, after dinner they would move to the drawing room

where the butler would serve tea. If, however, the meal was more formal, the ladies would 'withdraw', leaving the gentlemen to be served with port and cigars while they exchanged gossip and talked about business, before 'rejoining the ladies'.

At the end of the day, the butler would check that all doors and windows on the ground floor were secured, that all fires were dampened down or extinguished, and all lamps out.

## The butler's domain

Finally the butler would retire to his domain downstairs. At Tyntesfield in Somerset the butler occupied two rooms immediately behind the main stairs, perfectly placed to oversee the smooth running of the household. He had a pantry fitted with cupboards and a special wood-lined sink for washing precious and fragile objects. Next door was his bedroom, only accessible through the pantry. In the Victorian era, when fear of theft from great houses was quite common, considerable thought was given to the security of the highly portable household silver. As architect J.J. Stevenson advised in *House Architecture* of 1880:

*For the safety of the plate it is usual to place the butler's bedroom beside the pantry, the plate-safe or plate-room entering into the bedroom or, better, into a passage between them.*

Above: The Butler's Pantry at Cragside, Northumberland, showing the work benches and butler's equipment. This small room was used by the butler when on duty, providing privacy with easy access to the front door, kitchen, pantry, dining room and the other reception rooms.

# Dignity and discretion

Butlers were expected to accommodate the foibles of their employers with no response beyond the slightly raised eyebrow and the carefully inclined bow. Mrs Venetia James was an important Society hostess with a millionaire husband and a luxurious and lavishly appointed house in Grafton Street in London, yet was reputedly so mean that she filled her Friday dinner parties with notable Catholics so that she could economise on the provisions bills by only serving fish. She also instructed her staff to keep portion sizes to an absolute minimum. On one occasion, an entire dinner party had been given the component parts of a single fowl, thinly spread between many plates. Venetia passed a cryptic note to Went, her long-suffering butler. It read 'DCSC', which translated as 'Don't Cut Second Chicken'.

The grander the establishment, the more dignified the butler, who was expected to embody gravitas. The butler's appearance was carefully calculated to be immaculate, but slightly out of date. As a senior servant, he did not wear livery, but spent his daylight

Right: The butler's morning coat hanging in the Butler's Pantry in Florence Court. His outfit was designed to be formal, yet imperceptibly dated, so he could not be mistaken for a member of the gentry.

24

hours in a black morning coat, a dark waistcoat, a white shirt with a high-necked collar, a black tie and grey trousers, and on his evening shift wearing more formal black tie and tails. However, the suit would be of an almost imperceptibly dated cut and the butler would deliberately affect some glaring sartorial error, such as the 'wrong' tie fastened in an outmoded style, so that the socially acute could instantly identify his servant status. To be very tall was considered an immense asset to a butler, and was believed to add to his earning power. Eric Horne, a former footman and butler, who wrote two racy and highly entertaining accounts of life below stairs in *What the Butler Winked At* (1924) and *More Winks* (1933), bemoaned the fact that he was not tall enough to command a better salary.

The trusted butler was a model of discretion. Often party to confidential talk, the butler needed to be able to discriminate between moments when he should make his presence felt, and those when he should blend into the wallpaper, the better to absorb fascinating information.

*The butler and footmen who stood behind the dining-room chairs during lunch and dinner overheard social secrets and political scandals that today would make them a fortune from sales to the press. There is no reason to suppose that they ever repeated these titillating conversations to anybody. Their discretion was taken absolutely for granted...*

Ursula Wyndham, *Astride the Wall: A Memoir 1913–1945*, 1988

In 1911 in London, fashionable society was shaken to the core when *The Times* revealed that an unscrupulous female journalist working for a number of American papers had approached a particularly well-connected lady's butler and asked him to pass on snippets of gossip overheard at dinner parties and in servants' halls. 'Harriet' was especially interested in the activities of grocery millionaire Sir Thomas Lipton, Sir Ernest Cassel, who was the late King's financial adviser, and Mrs George Keppel, Edward VII's final mistress. She claimed that she often bought gossipy missives from a network of domestic servants, and recompensed them well. *The Times* editorial felt that this naked attempt to bribe servants was a threat to the privacy that should be taken for granted in the houses of the ruling classes. Other newspapers, whose readers were less well-heeled, dutifully echoed their condemnation, though it is noticeable that most of them were not averse to running gossip in their society pages, presumably provided by sharp-eared servants.

# The chef

## A prestige appointment

In grander British households, considerable prestige was attached to employing chefs, especially French ones. The French Revolution had caused a massive diaspora of specialist servants of all types, whose former masters and mistresses had been exiled if they were lucky, or imprisoned or guillotined if they were less fortunate. Among the emigrants were some of the greatest chefs of Europe, each one looking for a new billet, but determined to cling to their highly regarded professional status. Accustomed to providing ostentatious displays of skill and extravagance to cast glory on their former employers, the new French chefs taken on by the British aristocracy hit a cultural barrier. Mutual incomprehension resulted – the English 'milord' was happiest with a high intake of roasted or boiled animal protein of all sorts, as unadorned as possible. The French chef felt slighted if his master did not require sublime examples of his art and, as in the case of Felix, the French chef who joined the household of the Duke of Wellington, would resign if his most strenuous efforts were met with apparent indifference.

## Speciality chefs

Speciality chefs were employed by the grandest households – at Petworth the pastry chef was Signor Michel Milone, who created fabulous concoctions in the calm and cool of his pastry kitchen. Milone was described by his daughter Violet Margaret:

*A chef by profession, though his habiliments [outfit] of bowler hat, black coat and rolled umbrella could easily have dubbed him for a 'City Gent'. But we knew better, for secreted in various pockets were the choicest of leftovers…* charlotte russe, *leg of chicken, gooey gateaux – brought to us at night when we were abed.*

Diana Owen, *Petworth: The Servants Quarters*, 1997

At Petworth in the 1890s the chef was earning £120 a year (£7,186 today), an impressive salary. He could command ample assistance: a roasting chef and a pastry chef, a bevy of kitchen maids and a couple of scullery maids or boys. At Cliveden, one of the grandest houses in the land, the Astor family could rely upon the services of a French chef. Cliveden's chef had five kitchen maids, enabling him to turn out magnificent formal dinners for 50 or 60 people during the Season, and to feed house parties of 20 or 30 guests most weekends.

Cheshire's Lyme Park, famed for its cuisine and hospitality, retained the services of a Monsieur Perez, who was unusually popular with the other staff. Accounts survive of occasional ferocious arguments between him and his kitchen maids, usually resolved by M. Perez pronouncing '*Assez, assez*!' in an impressive baritone and retreating to his curtained cubbyhole off the kitchen. He was a commanding figure, always wearing scarlet leather top boots, a white tunic and the traditional chef's hat. Like other chefs, he suffered occasional frustration as his most wonderful creations provoked only benign indifference. On one occasion he served nothing for lunch but vast quantities of cold meat; when pressed for an explanation he exploded, 'All this beautiful meat! And no-one is eating it! Someone has to!'

## High salaries

In the 1890s at Penrhyn Castle, successive chefs were assisted by three kitchen maids and a number of scullery maids. Because of the many large-scale parties given, especially high wages were paid: in 1883, Samuel Owen of Penrhyn was rewarded with £150 a year, while the house steward, George Clarke, received £120 annually. By contrast the housekeeper, Elizabeth Johnson, received a mere £50 a year, with the kitchen maids earning between £12 and £24.

Below: The pastry chef and his staff in 1910 at Waddesdon Manor, Buckinghamshire. Many hands were needed to produce the large and lavish dinners that were served here.

# The cook

*We may live without poetry, music and art;*
*We may live without conscience, and live without heart;*
*We may live without friends; we may live without books;*
*But civilized man cannot live without cooks.*

Edward Bulwer-Lytton, *The Dinner Hour*, 1895

## Plain cooks and professed cooks

The title 'cook' encompassed a wide range of skills. 'Plain' cooks were capable of turning out straightforward meals, roasts and vegetables, soups and simple desserts, which sustained the middle-class family and their resident staff. 'Professed' cooks claimed superior skills, including mastery of complicated foreign dishes; they required a support staff of kitchen maids and scullery maids, and could produce a formal dinner of many courses for 12, 18 or even 24 guests. The typical professional cook in a grand house would be a woman in her forties, who had worked her way up through domestic service, starting in her teens as a scullery maid, progressing to kitchen maid, being taught 'on the job' and gradually acquiring specialist skills and knowledge.

## An essential member of staff

Any complex Victorian or Edwardian household was dependent on the vagaries of the cook. Disaster loomed if she was incapacitated or was inebriated (an occupational hazard). In an era when the only 'takeaway' food might be from an insalubrious pie or fish-and-chip shop, 'cook giving notice' was a considerable inconvenience.

The relationship between cook and her mistress was a delicate one, easily upset. For a society lady who entertained, the competence of the cook was a direct reflection on her own qualities, and could easily be the Achilles' heel of her social aspirations. Consequently the acquiring, accommodating and retaining of a decent cook was a constant source of worry, and the cook's rank within the household was high. Not only was a cook always referred to as 'Mrs', regardless of her marital status, she also often insisted on autonomy in the kitchen, even requiring advance notice if the mistress wished to visit her in her domain. Geraldine, Marchioness of Bristol, boasted that she had never set foot in the kitchens at Ickworth in Suffolk.

## The cook's day

The cook's day was a long one, though many humble tasks were carried out by junior staff. Awakened at about 6.30am with a cup of tea, she could expect to find that the junior staff had already stoked the kitchen fire, and heated the range in preparation for the servants' breakfasts. The servants ate at around 7.30am and the family would not arise until at least 9am, to be served their breakfast around 9.30 to 10.00am. The cook received all the necessary ingredients from the gardener, or the produce delivered by butchers and fishmongers, and by mid-morning, lunch preparations would be well under way.

Each morning there was an interview between mistress and cook, after breakfast 'upstairs' in the morning room, when they discussed all meal requirements, the marketing that needed to be done, the number of diners at each meal, and advance notice was given of meals to be prepared for later in the week – soup, for example, tasted better when it was made at least a day before consumption. Once a week, in households in which there was no housekeeper, the cook provided her 'books', records of her transactions with various tradesmen, for approval by the mistress.

Above: The Great Kitchen at Saltram, Devon. The kitchen was built in the late 1770s and has an open range with roasting spits (seen in the background) and a cast-iron closed range installed in 1885.

Most cooks were expected to work six-and-a-half days a week, turning out large, complex and impressive meals three or four times a day from a workplace that was excessively hot, badly lit, ill-equipped and inconveniently laid out. It is perhaps unsurprising that occasionally they succumbed to tippling – beer money was often supplied on top of the agreed wages. Cooks were not always reliable: on one occasion the Drewe family of Castle Drogo in Devon were provided with an entrée of baked beans and poached eggs, as the cook had 'gone off with a bottle'.

Below: The dry larder at Lanhydrock in Cornwall, filled with jars of pulses and spices, tins, cans and boxes of food.

# Cooks' equipment

Cooks occasionally found themselves in difficulties. At Dunster Castle in Somerset the family employed a very short, very stout Dutchwoman called Olga. The household had invested in a prototype chest freezer, in which they stored game. Sir Walter Luttrell recalled in an interview:

*One awful day, when the Clerk of Works happened to be down for something, I suppose he was going down for a cup of tea and couldn't find Olga, and so he wandered down trying to find out where she was – it was down this long, long passage, the game larder – and there was a pair of gigantic legs stuck out over the top, and he couldn't get her out, she had tipped over, and she was very nearly at death's door. So he had to come racing up to get the butler to come down, and between them they managed to drag her out. Otherwise, we'd have had one dead, large cook on our hands – in the deep freeze, which would have taken a lot of explaining…*

# Stalwart cooks

One cook ran her kitchen with particularly impressive skill. Mrs Sangster arrived at Ickworth in Suffolk as cook in 1906, and remained in place for the next 50 years, taking on the dual role of cook-housekeeper. She was remembered as a woman of unusual kindness and generosity, but her control of the household was rigid, and her exceptionally high standards as a cook made her an exacting mistress. Her culinary creations were legendary, and she kept her recipes secret. Mrs Sangster sent her kitchen maids out of the room when she was performing particularly difficult tasks. Before her arrival the cooks at Ickworth had changed fairly regularly. A cook with longevity was somewhat unusual, as people moved on from one household to another with reasonable frequency, to better their position or their terms and conditions.

# Finding a good cook

Finding a good cook was often a task to try the householder's patience – at Arlington Court in Devon, Miss Rosalie Chichester kept a notebook recording her recruitment of staff and their reasons for leaving, whether voluntarily or not. In writing of one cook, Mrs Carter, she noted, with evidently mixed feelings, 'Left May 21st – given notice, as no maid would stay with her – a good Cook.' Her summary of the brief career of a Mrs Merry, however, was withering. Miss Chichester noted that this cook left six weeks after arriving, as she was '…quite impossible – maids not properly fed, everything wasted, dirty and idle'.

## Cook's tips and nips

The cook was held primarily responsible for the quality of food in her care. In an era before refrigeration, reliable canning and deep freezes, this could be a fraught business. Most great houses provided separate storage areas for different types of food, so that cross-contamination was limited. Even so the professional cook had to take precautions to keep her provisions fresh. Uncooked meat would be sprinkled with ground ginger and pepper to deter flies; milk would be boiled before storage, a process that effectively 'pasteurised' it and prolonged its life.

For the unfortunate cook whose ingredients were 'on the turn', there were traditional remedies to help disguise the taste of food past its best. Joints of meat were run under cold water, steeped in camomile tea, vigorously rubbed with a clean cloth and then sprinkled with salt, before roasting. Charcoal in the boiling water, or a large portion of sugar, improved the flavour of 'borderline' fish; charcoal was also pushed into the stomach cavity of poultry, to absorb the natural by-products of quiet decay.

Because of their status and their nominal title of 'Mrs', cooks were rarely accused of having 'followers' in the manner of younger female staff members, but they were also adept at evading censure. One (possibly apocryphal) tale has the mistress of a smart London townhouse, short of change to reply to a telegram, calling downstairs to Cook to ask 'Do you have any coppers down there?' The reply came back, 'Yes, ma'am, but they are both my cousins…' Cooks were reputed to favour a man in uniform, firstly soldiers, and latterly policemen. They were also surprisingly popular as second wives for successful tradesmen who admired their financial *nous* and ability to drive a hard deal; they made excellent hoteliers and innkeepers. As George Meredith wrote in *The Ordeal of George Feverel* (1859), 'Kissing don't last; cookery do!'

Below: Advertisement for a type of stove (c.1900). The cook attracts many admirers – but do they admire her for herself alone, or for what she can produce with the help of her Wilson Cooker?

## Cook's notebooks and 'receipt' books

Cook's sitting room was an inner sanctum, a combined office, store and lair. Here the cook might relax in the afternoon, in the precious lull between lunch and afternoon tea. Cooks consulted recipe books but they usually prided themselves on not being seen to do so; they jealously guarded their own recipes and trade secrets. Until the mid-nineteenth century, cooks tended to keep their precious 'receipts' (recipes) in notebooks, jumbling together observations on how to jug a hare alongside methods for removing warts, or deterring moths. Mrs Hale Parker's handwritten *Book of Receipts*, written in 1876, still survives at Arlington Court in Devon and among its many idiosyncratic charms is a recipe for Sheepshead Soup.

By the middle of the 1860s, cookery had been revolutionised by a publishing phenomenon – the books that were to make Eliza Acton and Mrs Beeton household names to future generations. Ambitious cooks collected recipe books and works on household proficiency, and mistresses supplied their staff with them as required. The earliest to gain popular currency was written by the French chef Ude and was called *The French Cook: or the art of cookery developed in all its branches*, which was written in 1813. Dr William Kitchiner's *The Cook's Oracle*, published in 1840, claimed that his tome was unique in being based on the practical experience of a housekeeper. Eliza Acton's *Modern Cookery for Private Families* (1845) listed the amounts of ingredients needed for each recipe, a boon for the domestically vague.

It was Isabella Beeton's *Book of Household Management*, published in 1861, which provided the greatest practical advice to the middle-class household and its staff, because it provided thrifty tips, practical information on how many portions a particular recipe could supply and how to use up leftovers. In addition, the book's instructions on servants' duties, wages and working conditions helped to codify the relations between householders and their staff; on occasion, Mrs Beeton's writings were referred to as the arbiter in demarcation disputes and salary negotiations.

There were also socially superior publications aimed at cooks and chefs working in grander establishments. Charles Francatelli was the chief chef to Queen Victoria. He published his *Cook's Guide* in 1862, and it became a culinary classic throughout the next decades in country houses all over Britain. A well-thumbed copy survives at Lanhydrock and it is evident that successive cooks and chefs

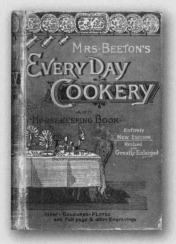

Above: Front cover of *Mrs Beeton's Every Day Cookery and Housekeeping*, published in 1890. Although Mrs Beeton died in her late 20s, her books, especially this one, have become legendary.

regarded its recommendations as sacrosanct. At Lanhydrock, soup was usually followed by fish, roast meats and side dishes, another meat course and as many as six further accompanying vegetables or puddings. Different wines would be served with each course.

### Training for cooks

Cooks often acquired superior skills through their own efforts in seeking training. Mrs Agnes Marshall opened her School of Cookery off Regent Street in London, where she gave practical demonstrations and teaching sessions to both cooks and their mistresses, from one-day courses to full apprenticeships. She also provided certificates and diplomas, which were highly prized by professional cooks as proof of their achievements. She published best-selling cookery books, sold kitchen implements and earned large sums by endorsing ranges and gas cookers.

Some cooks were lucky enough to have enlightened and well-connected mistresses. Mrs Isabella Menzies was the daughter of a head forester who worked on the estates of the Duke of Montrose. Her mother encouraged an early taste for cookery, sending her to learn the culinary arts at a well-known school in Atholl Crescent in Edinburgh. She was then engaged by Mrs Ronnie Greville at Polesden Lacey, who, whenever she dined out at the Ritz or the Savoy and came across a new dish of particular interest, would make arrangements for Mrs Menzies to learn the method, so that she could replicate it for her guests.

## Entertaining and the 'professed cook'

Producing a formal dinner for a large number of guests was a considerable challenge, even for the experienced 'professed cook'. Preparations would start days in advance, with negotiations between cook and mistress as to the menu, the ordering of the ingredients, and the inevitable discussions between butler or house steward, or even the master, as to which wines would be served with each course. At country houses, the head gardener was always consulted about the availability of seasonal vegetables or exotic fruit (a great coup for the hostess was to be able to say that the peaches or grapes were grown by 'our people' on the family estate). Mrs Greville, Edwardian hostess *par excellence*, would have dairy produce, vegetables, fruit and flowers delivered from her Polesden Lacey estate in Surrey to her Mayfair mansion during the London Season.

### Preparations

Down in the kitchens, the tension would build throughout the day. The competent cook ran her kitchen like a seasoned campaigner;

between the hours of 5 and 9pm, no superfluous conversation was allowed in the kitchen. Comparatively simple dishes such as roast meats were prepared by a competent kitchen maid, anxious to learn, so that in later years she too could be promoted to the position of cook. As the heat mounted and the pressure rose, scullery maids would prepare vast quantities of vegetables, often carved into intricate shapes or perfect spheres. The housekeeper might well have organised an impressive-looking *bombe* or ice for one of the desserts; the cook would keep one eye on the kitchen clock, as the butler upstairs in the drawing room discreetly dispatched a footman to gauge the situation down in the lower regions, standing by with an imperturbable expression until he got 'the nod'.

Above: The cook in a family kitchen, depicted in an advertisement for Liebig's Extract (c.1890)

## Dinner is served

Having been informed that all was ready, the butler would catch the eye of his hostess and announce in sonorous tones, 'Ladies and Gentlemen, dinner is served'. In the drawing room the guests would rouse themselves and progress in pairs to the dining room. Down in the kitchen serving staff would be dispatched up to the servery, a small room hidden by a jib-door leading to the dining room, to serve the first course, usually soup. The footmen would already be in place in the dining room, ready to slip a chair under a well-dressed rear, waiting for the signal from the butler. Dinner was under way, the mistress nervously making conversation with the guest of honour, the master being rogueishly charming to his principal female guest. Upstairs, all was calm and civilised. Meanwhile, 6m (20ft) below the dining room, in the hellish fury of the basement, the cook was barking orders and stirring frantically.

# The kitchen maid

Kitchen maids assisted the cook, preparing the food to be used, grinding spices in the pestle and mortar, chopping meat and herbs, making sauces and running to and from storerooms. They made gravies and soups, and boiled up bones to make stockpots. They filleted fish, plucked poultry and skinned rabbits; they kept an eye on joints roasting on spits, and often made the servants' meals and the food for all occupants of the nursery, both adult and juvenile.

As a kitchen maid, a young woman could train 'on the job' and learn to be a cook, a promising role for a bright and independent individual. They usually started as scullery maids, washing up dirty dishes and pans by hand. After perhaps a year, they might be allowed to wash and peel root vegetables; if they showed promise, the cook might promote them to second kitchen maid after a further year.

## The kitchen maid's duties

Below: The Household Staff (c.1900) at Treasurer's House, York.

Mary Luckey, one of a number of kitchen maids at Petworth in the 1890s, received £18 a year, the approximate equivalent of £1,078 today. Her duties included making breakfast for the other servants and buns for their tea, and her afternoons were spent cleaning the

kitchens and scrubbing the floors before preparing the vegetables for the family's dinner. The 'front of house' vegetables, those intended for 'upstairs', were sculpted into spheres, before being simmered in stock or butter. Mary's deputy, the second kitchen maid, prepared the regular vegetables to be consumed by the staff.

## A kitchen maid at Powis

The kitchen maid, vital though her role was, almost never saw the principal rooms of the house in which she worked. Despite spending two years working as a kitchen maid to the Earl and Countess of Powis at Powis Castle, 'C.M.B.' was only shown over 'the front part of the house' once. Sixty-eight years later, she could still recall the gigantic rooms with 'beautiful furniture, glass and china and enormous paintings in heavy gilt frames'.

There were two kitchen maids employed at Powis Castle in 1900, from an indoor staff of 29, and with 14 gardeners. The kitchen maids worked in support of the cook, usually cooking vegetables, roasting game, and generally acting as a 'spare pair of hands' for the cook. Preparation was crucial and a decent cook demanded that her working environment was perfectly equipped with everything she might need before she got under way. As C.M.B. recalled:

*My first job in the morning was to lay up the Kitchen table. This was quite a performance. The Cook and the first Kitchen maid sat opposite each other at the end of the table with their boards in front of them. Between the two there would be a box with all kinds of seasoning and another with cooking wines and sauces. Six large sheets of cartridge paper were opened and laid out and on these would be a bowl of potatoes, onions, lemons, bouquets and parsley and a quantity of eggs. Then, all laid in the proper way would be every sort of cooking spoons, forks, fish slices, a bundle of skewers, about six kitchen rubbers and some fish napkins.*

Archive account of 'C.M.B.' held at Powis Castle

## Helping Cook

The kitchen maid prepared materials and containers for bread-making, which was undertaken every afternoon, producing household bread and cakes. After breakfast was served upstairs and downstairs, the kitchen table was cleared by the kitchen maid and the preparations would be repeated for lunch and dinner. Meanwhile the cook and mistress would have agreed the dishes for that day's meals, and the kitchen maids would set to preparing and cooking it.

### Preparations for dinner

Immediately after lunch was served, extensive preparations began for dinner in the evening, a major undertaking if the family were entertaining. The kitchen staff ate their tea around 5pm so that they could concentrate fully on the preparations for dinner. Sauces and special dressings were made, and garnishes prepared; tureens and serving dishes were warmed ready to receive the various courses. Footmen lined up to carry the heavy trays up to the dining room.

After the meal, the serving dishes, glasses, cutlery and plates were brought back down to the kitchen, and the final mammoth task of the day began. The washing up generated by a formal six- or eight-course dinner, for perhaps fourteen people, could use a thousand separate items, each of which had to be washed by hand and treated with immense care. The cleanliness of the kitchen and utensils was looked upon as a mark of a well-run kitchen. The pans and metal utensils were scoured with a mixture of sand, salt and soap and the range black-leaded. With all this done, they would thankfully retire to bed, leaving the kitchen tidy and the range stoked ready for another day's cooking.

Below: The Kitchen Scullery at Lanhydrock, Cornwall. Slate-lined sinks were used for the preparation of vegetables and zinc-lined ones for washing up crockery and utensils.

## Working conditions

Conditions for kitchen maids improved a little as time went by, as they might be allowed some time off. Annie Evans started as a scullery maid at Penrhyn Castle, Gwynedd, in 1908, at the age of eighteen, and was eventually promoted to head kitchen maid, before leaving in 1927. Her basic working hours were 6am to 10.30pm, with the morning spent preparing for luncheon for 'upstairs', and dinner for 'downstairs'. Annie and her fellow kitchen maids occasionally had free time between 2.30 and 6.30pm. If the weather was good they might go into Bangor, or walk in the grounds. They could also spend the time relaxing or writing letters home, so long as they were ready by 6.30pm to resume work, preparing the family's dinner and then the staff's supper.

In time, the more arduous cleaning tasks, along with the washing up and the preparatory scrubbing of vegetables, would be undertaken by the scullery maids and the 'tweeny', or 'between' maid.

# The scullery maid
# and the tweeny

The word 'scullery' was derived from the Old French *escuelier*, a maker or seller of dishes; the term gradually came to mean the place where dishes, pots and plates were washed after use, by a scullion or scullery maid.

In the 1860s a scullery maid might earn £5 to £9 a year, a very low amount, equivalent to £215 to £388 today, but girls recognised that if they worked hard they stood a chance of being promoted.

## The trainee scullery maid

The trainee scullery maid was usually equipped with a pair of boots, several aprons, two print dresses, a few caps to cover her hair, a set of stays, some underwear, a flannel petticoat and a nightgown; in some parishes the vicar asked local philanthropic families to help equip young girls for their first jobs. On arrival she would be expected to share a room, often even a bed, with the lowliest kitchen maid, in a very basic room in the attics. After one or two years in the role, the scullery maid might be promoted to become kitchen maid.

## The scullery maid's duties

Most of the scullery maid's working life would be spent up to her elbows in water, either hot and greasy (washing up), or cold and muddy (scraping and peeling vegetables). Skinning and plucking animals was an unpleasant chore; experienced scullery maids would put the gamebird inside a deep bucket before commencing plucking, both to contain the feathers in case there was a sudden draught, and to stop the maggots escaping. The scullery maid helped to keep the kitchen clean at all times, a challenge in a busy and productive workplace – five wheelbarrow-loads of coal a day would be tipped into the stove to keep it going. She also had to clean all the copper pans with a mixture of salt, silver sand and vinegar.

## Life in the scullery

Hot water originated in the scullery, fuelled by the range, and was used for all washing purposes, carried in metal containers rather like watering cans to bedrooms and dressing rooms several times a day. The white cans were for cold water, and the copper cans for hot.

Above: Wooden drying racks and draining boards surround the sink in the Scullery at Uppark, West Sussex. This sink would have been used to wash pots and pans while delicate china and glass would be washed elsewhere.

In most houses, the scullery usually had a pair of sinks, located under the window for better visibility. One sink would be made of wood for the washing of chinaware, the other of stone for the more robust saucepans and similar equipment. All the kitchen's pots and pans, and the servants' china, would be washed in the scullery, while the family's precious dinner services and cutlery would be cleaned by the china-room staff or the footmen under the watchful eye of the butler. Next to the sinks was a wooden plate rack. The heat generated by the boiling coppers would dry plates and saucepans rapidly.

Equipment to help the scullery maid's daily chores was limited. Mrs Hale's handwritten *Book of Receipts*, dating from 1876, recommends making brushes for scouring saucepans '…from pine needles. Collect a number of the longer ones & bunch them together, so that the ends are evenly arranged. Place a stick about half way down the middle of the bunch, tie round securely & fasten with string.'

## The tweeny

The tweeny's name derived from her role as an 'inbetween maid', or general dogsbody; she would be expected to take on the least attractive tasks in the household, such as the muckier tasks in the nursery, or assisting the scullery maids, and she had very little status.

# The hall boy

The hall boy was employed to run errands for the butler and footmen, to tackle the dirtiest and heaviest jobs, such as chopping wood, cleaning the servants' boots and shoes, shovelling coal, disposing of the rubbish, moving furniture and taking messages or post to the nearby village. As his title suggests, he was normally found in the wide corridor that connected the servants' quarters in the basement, awaiting instruction.

The hall boy's accommodation usually consisted of a fold-down bed in the hallway, and he had almost no privacy. Typically, the household would recruit a young, local boy, preferably one who looked physically strong and was reasonably intelligent. This was the first rung on the menservants' career ladder; with application and discipline, not to mention luck, he might become an under-footman in a few years and might even be appointed butler in time.

Below: The trolleyway runs the length of the cellars at Tatton Park and was used to move the coal needed to keep the fires burning.

# The stillroom maid

The stillroom was originally used for the making of oils, potions and herbal remedies. It gained its name because it was where the mistress of the house distilled medicines or scents. By the late nineteenth century the housekeeper had taken over the room to oversee the making of coffee, jams, preserves and pickles, and for the preparation of afternoon teas for the gentry. At Penrhyn Castle in North Wales there were two stillroom maids listed in the wages book for 1883, and three by 1908. They made all the buns and cakes, and fresh rolls for breakfast.

Below: The Stillroom at Tatton Park was used during the Victorian period to prepare light meals.

Stillroom maids felt themselves to be separate from and superior to the kitchen and household staff; they wore their own clothes, rather than a uniform, and were less likely to get grubby or hot in the course of the working day. In pre-Victorian times, when the mistress was expected to be vigorous and self-reliant, the stillroom was very much her domain and laboratory.

# The stillroom maid's duties

At Petworth in Surrey the senior stillroom maid between 1879 and 1888 was called Mary Bell, and she was paid £18 a year, about £1,078 in modern money. She and her juniors reported to the housekeeper, and they were instructed in the preparation of preserved fruit and bottling fruit in alcohol, such as prunes in brandy, or sloe gin. They also provided non-alcoholic beverages and in summer would produce gallons of lemonade or barley water, a refreshing alternative to beer or wine, and increasingly popular as the Temperance Movement gained a grip on Victorian society.

The stillroom maids often had special responsibility for the care of the best china, the exquisite dinner services and the matching serving dishes, and the very fine tea and coffee services.

## Jams, bottling and pickling

The housekeeper directed the stillroom maids in the making of vats of jam and pickles for future consumption, using the produce of the estate. Jams were made using loaf sugar, moulded into the shape of a large cone, each one of which could weigh 2.2–16kg (5–35lb). To break chunks off the cone, the maids used 'sugar nippers', rather like large pliers with a cutting edge. In addition, the stillroom maids would bottle or dry fruit from the estate as soon as it was available. Cherries were bottled in brandy, or whole strawberries in Madeira wine and sugar. Apricots could be dried in the oven and stored.

Adventurous housekeepers would attempt to pickle all sorts of garden produce, from cabbages to walnuts. Pickled onions and gherkins were highly popular, and spicy chutneys influenced by contact with the Indian sub-continent were prized; piccalilli used mustard seeds to achieve a sensation of heat. Capers were collected and bottled for caper sauce, which added piquancy to cooked mutton. Most housekeepers also had their own recipe for various forms of 'catsup', later known as ketchup, a semi-liquid flavouring to be added to soups and stews to add depth; mushroom ketchup was a particularly handy favourite, while Mrs Beeton advocated the steeping of 50 fresh chillies in vinegar, which sounds lethal.

Surprising to modern sensibilities was the need to pickle eggs too, but hens naturally go 'off lay' over the winter, and therefore in the nineteenth century eggs were imported to Britain between December and the end of February, with consequent high prices and an effect on their freshness. Canny housekeepers therefore stored excess summer eggs in vast jars filled with limewater.

Above: Well into the twentieth century sugar came in cones which could be up to 1m (3ft) tall and 35cm (14in) in diameter at the base. This sugar cone is in the kitchen at Saltram, Devon.

# The housekeeper

To Mary Webster, housekeeper at Erddig in Clwyd, who died in 1875:

*Upon the portly form we look*
*Of one who was our former Cook,*
*No better keeper of our Store*
*Did ever enter at our door.*
*She knew, and pandered to our taste,*
*Allowed no want and yet no waste.*
*And for some thirty years or more*
*The cares of Office here she bore…*

Philip Yorke, owner of Erddig, 1911

In middle-class homes, the overseeing role fell to the mistress, who might delegate the management of the female staff to the cook. But in households where sufficient finances were available and a lady's social obligations demanded much of her time, the trusted housekeeper was her agent and reported to her.

*As second in command in the house, except in large establishments, where there is a house steward, the housekeeper must consider herself as the immediate representative of her mistress, and bring, to the management of the household, all those qualities of honesty, industry, and vigilance, in the same degree as if she were at the head of her own family. Constantly on the watch to detect any wrong-doing on the part of any of the domestics, she will overlook all that goes on in the house, and will see that every department is thoroughly attended to, and that the servants are comfortable, at the same time that their various duties are properly performed.*

Isabella Beeton, *Mrs Beeton's Book of Household Management*, 1861

# The duties of the housekeeper

Housekeepers were persons of authority and integrity; many of them remained in post for decades, and they were given the courtesy title of 'Mrs' whether married or not. The housekeeper wore no uniform; her quiet authority, sober appearance and enormous bunch of keys, known as a *châtelaine*, was enough to make her instantly recognisable. She engaged and dismissed housemaids, and taught new recruits their jobs. She oversaw the storerooms and linen supply, and often controlled all the provisioning too, with the exception of fresh produce, presenting her books once a week to the mistress for her approval. In well-ordered houses, both the housekeeper and the mistress preferred to settle the bills promptly as any discrepancy or complaint about the quality of the supplies would then be fresh in their minds.

## The housekeeper's room

The housekeeper at Sudbury Hall in 1871 was Esther Price from Herefordshire, who was 44 years old. As second-in-command of the household she was responsible for the welfare of those female servants who did not report to the cook, the 23 assorted maids and two laundry maids. She also had her own room. In many houses, the housekeeper's sitting room was known as 'Pug's Parlour', supposedly because the disapproving facial expression of its

Left: Mary Webster, housekeeper at Erddig, Wrexham, during the mid-nineteenth century.

Below: The Housekeeper's Room at Uppark, West Sussex.

occupant reminded the lower orders of pug dogs, then popular as lapdogs for elderly ladies. The room was usually large and comfortable. Drawing on his knowledge of Uppark, where his mother had been housekeeper, H.G. Wells described the housekeeper's room in his novel *Tono-Bungay* (1909):

*The much cupboarded, white-painted, chintz-brightened housekeeper's room where the upper servants assembled [and where] there was an old peerage and a Crockford together with the books of recipes, the Whitaker's Almanack, and the eighteenth century dictionary…*

### Practical knowledge

The housekeeper was expected to understand accounts and the principles of cooking, although she rarely interfered in the running of the kitchen, beyond ordering dry goods, such as flour, as required. Her duties included dealing with tradesmen and setting the pattern of work throughout the year, for example, timetabling the spring cleaning and interior decoration.

A good housekeeper had a practical knowledge that roamed across many fields, including basic first aid, such as distilling willow bark as a remedy for headaches. For these recipes, she might have a collection of handwritten notebooks of her own, or she might rely on classic published works, such as *Mrs Beeton's Book of Household Management* (1861) or *Cassell's Household Guide* (1880). She would know how to deal with an infestation of moths in a clothes cupboard (the interior should be rubbed with a strong decoction of tobacco, followed by treatment with spirits of camphor) or how to remove white spots from varnished furniture using the fumes from a warming pan.

### Care of household linen

Right: The China Closet in the Housekeeper's Passage at Tatton Park in Cheshire, including part of a 900-piece nineteenth-century French glass service. The housekeeper was responsible for the household china, in addition to her many other duties.

The care of the household linen was a crucial role: the housekeeper was expected to buy it, stock-take it, care for it and store it on carefully labelled shelves in linen presses or cupboards. There were three main categories of linen in any grand household: 'best', 'family' and 'servants'. Housekeepers were advised to institute a cyclical system to ensure even wear within each category, and to 'demote' worn textiles from one category to the next when necessary. Linen would be checked on its return from the laundry and set aside for repairs if necessary. The housekeeper accumulated piles of mending and then allocated it to one of the housemaids on a relatively quiet afternoon. Bed sheets for servants, which were

worn in the centre, would be slit lengthways, re-seamed 'sides to middle', and re-hemmed to extend their useful life. Eventually the remnants would be used as dusters or sold as rags for making paper.

## The housekeeper's domain

Housekeepers considered themselves custodians of the fabric of country houses, and could be very protective of their domain. Mrs Campbell, housekeeper at Lyme Park in the Edwardian era, would meet workmen at the back door to the house and insist they change their hob-nailed boots for carpet slippers (which she provided) before they could enter the building. The housekeeper also acted as a quartermaster for the domestic supplies required by the household. She held the key to the storeroom in which were kept bulk supplies of flour, rice, tea and coffee. Soap and candles were also stored here – both were believed to improve in quality if stored for a long time, so an organised housekeeper would stockpile candles made in spring for use the following winter.

The housekeeper supervised the annual cleaning session, often in May, a time when the family would be absent, travelling abroad or staying in one of their other properties. She supervised other staff in cleaning the house from top to bottom, leaving furniture and fittings spotless and protected against dust and dirt, vermin and sunlight, until the family returned. Among the many other duties, the housekeeper would supervise the inventory and care of china. At Petworth, Ivy Richardson reminisced:

*Once a year all the china was taken out of the cabinets and carefully washed. Florence Roper supervised but we did the washing. I can still tell good china just from the feel of it. No, I never broke any and I knew to look for repairs, you didn't wash that part in case you dissolved the gum...*

Above: *Mrs Garnett, Housekeeper* by Thomas Barber at Kedleston Hall, Derbyshire.

At Petworth in the 1860s, housekeeper Mrs Lingford married the bailiff, Smith; she was responsible for all the china and linen stores, and for the laundry maids and housemaids at both the London house and the country estate. She stayed at Petworth most of the year, and to oversee the annual spring clean. However, she would make occasional trips to London to oversee the family's staff in the London house, and to make purchases.

# Powerful housekeepers

Housekeepers came from a variety of more lowly roles. Sarah Neal, the daughter of a Chichester innkeeper, had been the lady's maid to Frances Bullock, sister to Lady Fetherstonhaugh of Uppark. Sarah left to marry, but returned to employment there in 1880 as the housekeeper, accompanied by her youngest son, Bertie. He later became a writer; as H.G. Wells, he disguised the house as 'Bladesover' in his 1909 novel *Tono-Bungay*. The author thought that his mother '...was perhaps the worst housekeeper that was ever thought of'.

The powerful housekeeper, the repository of a family's secrets, could be an intimidating and even terrifying figure. Although *Rebecca* (1938) by Daphne du Maurier falls outside the period covered by this book, it is notable how the unnamed heroine defers to, and is manipulated by, Mrs Danvers, the maddened chatelaine of Manderley, rabidly loyal to a long-dead mistress. Less extreme instances did occur in real life: Lady Bristol told her granddaughter that she had been terrified of the housekeeper at Ickworth, a Mrs Parish, who had control of every aspect of the day-to-day running of the household. When Mrs Parish retired in 1907, the Marchioness did not replace her, but instead promoted the popular and impressive Mrs Sangster to the post of cook-housekeeper.

However, most housekeepers were regarded with affection and respect by the families who employed them. Lady Maud Baillie, who was born in 1896, remembered her childhood at Hardwick Hall near Chesterfield warmly:

*The housekeeper, an awe-inspiring little woman dressed in black silk, reigned supreme. She had a real love and a deep pride in the house. On one occasion, when asked if the house was haunted, she replied that once or twice Bess of Hardwick, who died some 350 years ago, had come to thank her for her care of the house, but, she added, 'Of course there are no ghosts.'*

By the Edwardian era, the practice of employing housekeepers had spread from the aristocracy to the upper middle classes; competent and efficient women were often taken on by householders to run their homes. Thanks to new labour-saving devices they were able to do this with fewer supporting staff. A respectable position in a decent home, with comfortable accommodation and a salary, was now available to women who previously might have struggled to survive on their own.

# The housemaid

The housemaid's lot was a tough and physical job, which she was expected to undertake with a certain amount of delicacy and discreet behaviour. In large households, the work she undertook might be spread among other staff, but in smaller places she faced a Herculean task every day.

## The housemaid's duties

Succinctly described by Clive Aslet as 'a foot soldier in the Victorian household's constant war against grime' (*The English House*, 2008), her role was essentially to keep the house clean and tidy, so that everything would be perfect for the family. Usually the first member of the household to rise in the morning, in summer between 5 and 6am, and in winter nearer to 6.30am, the housemaid would open the shutters, put down protective druggets to cover the carpets, then clean out the grates of the dining room and sitting room. Each fireplace needed to be thoroughly cleaned and polished every day, and the ashes removed. Having relaid and lit the fires, she would sweep and dust each room, polish the brass, clean the lamp glasses and candlesticks, brush the stair carpets and front hall, sweep the front steps and buff up the front-door knocker. She lit fires in dressing rooms upstairs and began to carry up copious amounts of hot water to the bedrooms, so that the family could variously bathe or wash. A brief breakfast was followed by a race against time, to stock up coal buckets before any gentleman of the family emerged on to a corridor or staircase and was put in the embarrassing position of having to consider offering assistance to a female grappling with a heavy burden, even if she was of a lower class.

*…Clean houses are the pride and boast of England; housemaids, too, who know their duty and take a pride in doing it…*

'Duties of the Housemaid', *The Servants' Magazine*, February 1857

### Bedroom duties

While the family was breakfasting, the housemaid discreetly removed wash basins and chamber pots from the bedrooms, carrying them downstairs (using the servants' staircase if one existed), to empty, scour and return by the same route. In the bedrooms, housemaids grappled daily with turning heavy mattresses, remaking beds, plumping pillows and bolsters, and sweeping under the bed.

They would also check for bedbugs, which, if found, would necessitate taking the whole bed and its frame apart and vigorously scrubbing all components. Once a week, the carpets would be turned back and the floors swept; smaller carpets, such as hearthrugs, which accumulated a residue of cinders and dust, were carefully rolled and removed to be beaten outside.

## Tidying downstairs

Once the bedrooms were clean and tidy, the housemaid would move through the other downstairs rooms, dusting and cleaning as required, possibly lighting further fires in, for example, the master's study. The conscientious housemaid had to be careful not to disturb any papers, and books and ornaments had to be replaced exactly where they had been left. It was believed that the disastrous burning of the first manuscript of Carlyle's great text, *The French Revolution* (1837) had been due to the over-zealous tidying up of the housemaid at the home of the author's friend, John Stuart Mill. The dusting and tidying of all writing desks would normally be undertaken by the butler, a more trusted figure in the household hierarchy. Footmen were deputed to clean the more vulnerable items such as ornaments and pier glasses. Throughout the morning, the housemaid would also be obliged to answer both front and back doorbells if they rang, first discarding her work apron and putting on a clean one to answer the front door. Lunch was followed by a welcome change of pace; she could put on a clean black gown and sit down at last to concentrate on her mending and darning. Naturally she would have to answer ringing bells, both internal and external, before helping to prepare the table for dinner.

Below: Housemaid's closet at Dunham Massey in Cheshire (c.1906).

## Evening duties

Then came the laborious business of transporting numerous cans of hot water from the basement to the family's bedrooms, for baths, shaving and washing. The water cans would be refilled with dirty water and the maid would carry them back down to the kitchen and dispose of their contents there.

While the family was dining, the housemaid would eat supper in the servants' hall, and then check the drawing room was perfect and the fire well stoked. Before the family retired for the night, the housemaid would light bedroom fires and take up warming pans or hot-water bottles if required to air the beds. She would refill the jugs on the washstand in each bedroom with warm water, and wait patiently for the family to retire.

## The cleaning ritual and housemaid's knee

As well as the daily round, each day had its allocated cleaning ritual: all carpets needed sweeping once a week with damp tea leaves to remove dust. Damp salt was a popular treatment for carpets at Petworth in West Sussex, and Ivy Richardson, recalled 'It was amazing how black the salt became.' Wallpaper was rubbed with old crusts of bread to remove grubby fingerprints. The silver frequently needed cleaning, as it tarnished quickly in polluted air; the windows needed frequent washing. Bursitis, an inflammation of the joints caused by repetitive movements, was an occupational hazard known by the appropriate name of 'housemaid's knee', or 'tennis elbow', depending on which part of the body it affected.

The housemaid was required to keep her hands as clean as possible; a difficult task in an era of black-leading, coal-fire lighting and brass polishing, which nevertheless had yet to invent protective rubber gloves for household tasks. Sensible housemaids invested in a cheap pair of leather gloves, to protect their hands.

The workload of the typical housemaid was impressive, especially at the larger country houses. At Stourhead in Wiltshire, for example, there were 42 fireplaces, and on a cold winter's day they would consume over a ton of coal, the equivalent of 135 bucket-loads transported by a small team of housemaids, a total of 4,800 steps. Nowadays Stourhead is heated by an oil-fired central-heating system, controlled by a single switch.

Below: The castered tin bath in the Silk Dressing Room at Tatton Park, Cheshire. The bath was filled with hot water by maids and it was kept warm by a coal fire in the firebox at the bottom of the bath.

## The housemaid's tools

The housemaid's tools were fairly rudimentary in the Victorian era, consisting mostly of brushes of every possible variety, mops and cloths. Old bristle toothbrushes were treasured because they were so useful, robust enough to use on the curlicues of ornate staircases, or the tricky corners of wooden carvings.

It is salutary to think how many generations of housemaids must have applied a certain amount of vigour, if not Vim, to the exquisite, irreplaceable Grinling Gibbons carvings at Petworth. A publication of 1877 entitled *The Housemaid: Her Duties and How to Perform Them*, advised housemaids to use only a very soft, clean, dry duster on the surface of paintings. The more robust line of a previous era recommended that venerable oil paintings were dabbed with a weak linseed-oil solution on a cloth, or treated to a wash with diluted gin. Magnificent marble sculptures, from The Vyne in Hampshire to Kedleston Hall in Derbyshire, were treated with '…a sponge with soda, then with soft soap', according to Ivy Richardson.

Above: Advertisement for a commercial cleaning product (c.1900). Bagley's Furniture Paste polish was one of a raft of products that began appearing during the period.

The three housemaids at nearby Sudbury Hall made their own furniture polish, a mixture of beeswax and turpentine, and they scrubbed the floors with sand mixed with beer. There were few commercially produced detergents or polishes; blocks of soap or scouring powders were the main cleaning agent, while soda crystals were used for tough jobs. By the Edwardian era, there were some commercial cleaning products such as Brasso, which made specific jobs easier. In addition, the arrival of the Ewbank carpet sweeper was a great boon to housemaids – with this lightweight and almost soundless device, carpets could be freed from grit and lint in moments. The first suction vacuum cleaner was marketed in Britain in 1901, but its adoption was a slower process; firstly the house needed a reliable electricity supply, and secondly some householders refused to accept that cleaning could be conducted in anything other than total silence. But some employers were more far-sighted – at Castle Drogo in Devon there was an ingenious vacuum-cleaning system, incorporated into the very fabric of the building. Each room had a suction vent into which a vacuum cleaner could be fitted; when operated, the housemaid could collect and dispose of the dust and fluff in an instant, all the detritus being collected centrally.

*The duty of the housemaid is to sweep and clean the rooms, arrange the bedrooms, and attend to their fires. As her work is throughout the house, there is in many cases no special apartment for her use; but both on the principle that each servant should have her own place to work in, and from their great convenience, a housemaid's closet should be provided in every house with any pretension to good planning… to save the labour of carrying water up or down stairs, there should be a housemaid's closet on each floor, near the servants' stair or in some retired corner among the bedrooms, so that slops do not have to be carried up or down stairs or along corridors.*

J.J. Stevenson, *House Architecture*, vol II, 1880

Below: Bellows, a coal scuttle and other fire irons in the parlour of the 1870s house at the Birmingham Back to Backs.

## The housemaid's closet

Small storerooms on each floor allowed the housemaids to keep their cleaning materials conveniently close. At Tyntesfield, on the first and second floors were rooms where the housemaids could fill the bedroom jugs with hot and cold water morning and evening, a labour-saving and efficient arrangement. More fortunate housemaids also had a coal closet on each floor, where they could maintain a supply of coal, kindling and matches in order to be able to light fires.

### Fire duties

Lighting fires was a skilful if dirty task, for which the housemaid put on a dark-brown apron to protect her clothes from dust and ashes, and laid a drugget over the area around the grate to minimise the mess. First the ash and cinders had to be raked out and placed in a cinder box, and then a new pile of coal and wood would be built up in a pyramid and lit with a safety match. If the materials were damp, the fire might be slow to catch and the housemaid could be held up in her busy schedule, trying to coax life into a recalcitrant grate. A sheet of newsprint could be used to 'draw' a slow fire; holding the whole sheet against the surrounding hearth, close to the flames, caused the fire to flare up as the ambient oxygen was used up and the flames drew oxygen down the chimney. This procedure was risky – it was very easy for the newspaper to catch light, and the maid had to be alert to evade injury.

Throughout the day it was the housemaid's responsibility to check that all the fires in use were burning successfully, to replenish the fuel and refill the coal scuttles. A full coal scuttle could easily weigh 13.5kg (30lb), which was the same as a bath can of hot water.

# The lady's maid

By the early Victorian era, the mistress of any wealthy and fashionable household was expected to be a decorative figurehead, a model of genteel behaviour and ladylike pursuits, preferably involving 'good works'. To maintain an immaculate appearance, she needed assistance – someone whose whole energies would be poured into helping her into and out of the complex costumes expected of her rank. In an era of advanced prudery about the human body and its functions, it is perhaps surprising to consider the level of intimacy necessitated by the close proximity of the mistress and the lady's maid.

The lady's maid often trained as a dressmaker or hairdresser before entering domestic service. Neat and self-reliant, literate and socially confident, she combined tact and discretion with a cheerful disposition. A hardy constitution was vital as the hours were long, and the necessary travel could be arduous. The lady's maid accompanied her mistress when she went to stay at other houses. There her relative position in the hierarchical servants' hall would be dictated by the status of her mistress. Careful of her virtue with charming footmen and frisky friends of the family, she needed to be totally trustworthy, as she would have to guard her mistress's jewels, as well as her secrets.

*The lady's maid was a feared figure in the household. Fashionable women, who felt the need to have their maid about them to help with their hair-styling, made confidantes of these invaluable assistants and, since confidences are apt to run in two directions, it was feared the lady's maid would report on any little peccadilloes being enacted on the far side of the baize door.*

Ursula Wyndham, *Astride the Wall: A Memoir 1913–1945*, 1988

The lady's maid was provided with her own carpeted bed-sitting room on one of the upper storeys, and she was allocated a lower servant to clean it. At Stourhead in Wiltshire the lady's maid was important enough to have a very well-appointed bedroom, with a hip bath, washstand, ottoman, and Japanese screen, plus a tailor's dummy, a sewing machine and an extra electric socket for an iron – she was expected to work here too. The lady's maid could take her meals in 'Pug's Parlour', the housekeeper's room.

THE FASHIONS

Expressly designed and prepared for the

Englishwoman's Domestic Magazine.

AUGUST 1860

## French maids

In the higher echelons of British society, French lady's maids were fashionable, but they were thought to be volatile in nature, accustomed to a general level of extravagance, fashionable dress and high society, which the less energetic British gentlewoman found daunting. Swiss maids were regarded as steadier and less over-stimulating, and for a society lady travelling overseas, a francophone maid was an asset:

*There can be no possible doubt that every woman should have a French maid – there is no use in an English one. Directly the vista of abroad opens itself before us the English becomes merely an incubus, out-of-place, awkward, and incapable, too ill to move; while the French one, or the Swiss, will coquette with the railway porter, to the ultimate advantage of her mistress's belongings, and will pack and unpack with an absence of fuss, invariably the principal characteristic of the British-born body-servant.*

Mlle. Sans-Gêne, 'Notes from my Diary', *Country Life*, February 1897

## The duties of the lady's maid

The primary role of a lady's maid was to turn out her mistress in a state of fashionable perfection on all occasions. Any lady with social pretensions was expected to change her outfit six times a day, so the lady's maid was an essential presence. In fact, many women were completely incapable of dressing or redressing themselves. In the

Victorian era, most outfits were designed to button, lace or fasten at the back. Then there were the practical difficulties of the swaying, flexible steel crinoline or petticoat frame, or the later birdcage-like contraption, the bustle. Multiple petticoats trimmed with lace added volume underneath the skirt. By the Edwardian era, skirts were less bulky, but elegant formal blouses also buttoned at the back, and the neck of the garment might be boned up to the jaw-line, to encourage the correct posture, further constricting movement. The corsets were longer and more flat-fronted, which made them easier to wear while standing for a long time, though even less flexible when sitting down. Silk stockings were fastened to the corset's suspenders, and crotchless or 'trapdoor' cotton bloomers were worn so that ladies could use the loo without having to get completely undressed.

## Hairdressing and hats

By the turn of the century, the fashion was for ladies to wear their long hair very full, and to achieve the required density, considerable artifice was needed. The hair needed a suitably robust texture; so the lady's maid would apply talcum powder to her mistress's dry hair, to absorb some of the grease and bulk it out. Then strands of hair would be fixed over small fabric-covered pads, known as 'rats'; inventive maids even collected their mistress's discarded hair from combs and brushes to make 'rats' to match her natural hair exactly.

On top of this complex edifice, the Edwardian lady of fashion would add an enormous hat when going out into society. The management of one's headgear brought its own problems: Arthur Thompson, the young groom at Polesden Lacey in Surrey in the Edwardian era, recalled the logistical problems getting fashionable lady visitors safely in and out of horse-drawn carriages:

*When they came down, they'd have skirts out here, and bustles, and their hats – one lady couldn't get into the brougham. I had to take her to the station; she had a hat on as wide as that; she had to take her hat off to get into the brougham. The butler helped her in. I helped her out when we got down to the other end. She got out sort of sideways…*

Left: Fashion plate from *The Englishwoman's Domestic Magazine*, August 1860. Women with any social status wore tight corsets, crinolines and full skirts, even when riding.

Below: A French lady's maid helps her mistress with her toilette (1847).

## The mistress's care and comfort

In the evening the lady's maid occupied herself with sewing alterations and running repairs, cleaning jewellery or removing spots from clothes, while waiting for her lady's return – in the faster social circles, the hostess might not retire until 3 or 4 in the morning, and the lady's maid had to wait up for her, to undress her, put away her clothes and brush her hair, before she could go to bed herself.

The care and maintenance of the wardrobe of a lady of fashion was an absorbing business. The lady's maid was charged with storing all the clothes and accessories carefully while ensuring they were easy to find when required. Hanging was only suitable for light dresses in regular use; most garments were carefully folded and wrapped in linen cloths and stored in drawers and trunks. Furs were kept cool and free of moths; Cragside in Northumberland had close-fitting lead-lined wardrobes for the storage of furs. Summer and winter clothes were stored separately, often in camphor-lined trunks.

Below: The dressing table in Miss Rosalie Chichester's bedroom at Arlington Court, Devon.

Robust leather luggage and portmanteaux were used for the transport of clothes and accessories. When travelling with her mistress, the efficient lady's maid kept notes on the whereabouts of garments and accessories, so as to provide well-matched outfits for every occasion at short notice.

## A vital companion

On occasions, the lady's maid had to act with discretion. When the mistress was pregnant, the maid would advocate specially designed corsets and would monitor her health. Maids were also very protective of their employers, to conceal their foibles. Lady Jessica Sykes, for example, a society beauty, separated from her husband and was living in London where she developed an alcohol problem. Her faithful maid, Gotherd, had to hide the scent bottles as the mistress would drink those if nothing else was available, and she also resorted to concealing Madam's stays to prevent her from getting dressed, going out and disgracing herself in public.

Physical welfare and maintenance included assisting the lady with her bath, plucking eyebrows or touching-up grey roots. A good lady's maid had a battalion of beauty treatments and recipes to address every problem. She was also on hand when the mistress undertook some bracing health treatment, such as sea-bathing, or to accompany her lady to a 'cure' at some European spa, such as Baden-Baden or Biarritz. On occasions, the lady's maid had to administer first aid; in the case of hysterics, she was advised to mix 30 drops of laudanum with 30 drops of ether, followed by a glass of wine or cold water, which was undoubtedly effective.

On any overseas trip, the lady's maid acted as a constant companion, a ready-made chaperone and a source of entertainment. Her education was usually superior to that of the ordinary female servant. Mrs Greville, Edwardian society hostess and doyenne of Polesden Lacey, treated her maid as a companion:

*Though she loved power, she was not really a snob. This was proved by her relationship with her personal maid, whom she always called 'The Archduchess'. The title was apt; the Archduchess, who was deeply devoted to her mistress, had a natural distinction. One day I walked into the ground floor of the Café Royal and saw Maggie, in a plain black dress, sitting in a corner dining with the Archduchess. There was nothing incongruous or embarrassing about it. Why should there be? The two women were not only mistress and maid, they were best friends.*

Beverley Nichols, *Sweet and Twenties*, 1958

The close relationship with the mistress could provoke jealousy among other servants. Gossip from 'downstairs' occasionally reached the ears of the mistress, and the lady's maid was often suspected of being the conduit. In return, the lady's maid had to maintain her discretion or risk losing her job. Party to conversations between her mistress and her husband, she could gauge the state of the marriage, inevitably knowing an awful lot about the physical details of their relationship.

## Lady's maid's perks

As a matter of course, a lady's maid received her mistress's clothing cast-offs, which she would usually sell to specialist second-hand clothes shops. Damaged or *démodé* articles of clothing and accessories found a ready market among the aspirational lower classes. Some maids were also bribed by a haberdasher's or millinery firm, who would offer a handsome commission if fashionable ladies were persuaded to patronise their establishments.

## The long-term prospects of the lady's maid

Each lady's maid was aware that she had to maintain her own youthful looks and figure, as mistresses preferred a young and pretty acolyte. A few graduated to the role of housekeeper, but the nature of their specialised experience in service meant that they knew little about running a complex organisation 'below stairs'.

One possible route out was marriage, and as ladies' maids were generally good-looking, well dressed and with a veneer of sophistication, they were in demand among the more ambitious male servants. Elizabeth Hale served as a lady's maid at Erddig from 1848 to 1858, before marrying William Stevenson, the footman. Mr and Mrs Hale had saved money during their period in service, and they were able to invest it in their future lives. They moved to Brighton where they ran a superior lodging house, a task for which they would have been well suited, given their experience and organisational abilities. Elizabeth lived to a great age; born in April 1816, she died a centenarian in August 1916.

However, some lady's maids found it difficult to find a suitable husband. Attractive lady's maids might win the attentions of one of the men of the family, but servants' manuals and magazines warned firmly against the unhappy consequences almost certain to arise from such transgressive liaisons. However, it was not unknown for aristocrats to be smitten: Sir Henry Harpur of Calke Abbey in Derbyshire defied convention by marrying a lady's maid in 1792.

# The valet

The word 'valet' has come to mean a gentleman's personal servant, but in medieval terms it defined a youth living in a superior household so that he could learn courtly manners and practices from his social betters, improve his general education and contacts and acquire a little finesse.

A 'gentleman's gentleman' did not wear livery and, according to the wits, was only distinguishable from his master by the fact that he was often better dressed and had more pleasant manners. Footmen or butlers might stand in as a valet when required, laying out clothes and running baths for their masters or male household guests, but a fully fledged valet was a desirable status symbol.

## The duties of the valet

The valet acted like an *aide de camp*; he accompanied his employer on trips and visits, and assisted him on shoots and excursions, loading his guns or carrying his waterproof clothing. He made any journey go smoothly, by calling cabs, consulting rail timetables, and taking charge of the luggage. He shaved the master, usually making up his own special soap to do so, and would trim his hair. In all aspects of a gentleman's life, from arranging for flowers to be sent to a lady friend, to lying valiantly about the master's whereabouts to creditors, the resourceful valet was on hand to make it run as smoothly as clockwork.

Above: An elderly gentleman, desperate to regain the figure of his youth, has his valet lace him into a corset (1910).

Valets kept their master's clothes in top condition, pressing, cleaning and repairing the master's extensive wardrobe. Cynics might note that as the eventual cast-offs were given to the valet as a matter of course, it was worthwhile lavishing loving care on his future investment. Like the lady's maid, the successful valet knew numerous 'tricks of the trade' to clean and restore to freshness his master's clothes. He might be obliged to get sea-water stains out of hats (immerse the hat briefly in cold clean water, brush it immediately all over, following the direction of the nap, then hang it to dry on a peg), or have to waterproof a pair of leather shoes (apply a mixture of warm beeswax and mutton suet to the uppers and around the stitching). Meticulous to a fault, valets made themselves indispensable to their masters: not only did Sir Henry Hoare's man burnish his riding boots to an incredible shine, he also used the

Right: Shoes, boots and spats and cleaning materials in the Brushing Room at Newton House, Dinefwr. Meticulous valets kept their master's clothes in top condition.

shinbone of a deer to polish the inside of each boot, to make the surface exceptionally smooth.

The valet needed to be personable enough to get on with other servants when he and his master were staying at a strange house, so that he could use the facilities. At Stourhead, for example, there was all that was required for getting the worst of the mud off sporting clothes, including a 'breeches-cleaning dripping board… with lead-lined trough at the end for the waste', but it was located in the boot-and-knife man's room in the basement, so the valet needed the co-operation of other staff to find it.

Professionally pleasant, valets' impressive social skills led to occasional romances with their female colleagues. Lord Egremont's valet, Owen, married one of the ladies' maids at Petworth in the 1860s. Even Lady Violet Greville, a waspish observer of the social scene and outspoken critic of most of the servant classes (indeed, every class) had a soft spot for a decent valet:

*The gentleman's gentleman remains a unique specimen of high civilisation acting upon a naturally uneducated nature. There is veneer, but no real value, underneath. Yet, take him all in all, the gentleman's gentleman is agreeable to live with, easy to manage, unobtrusively useful, faithful as far as his lights go, devoted to what he thinks your interests and his, amiable and good-tempered, light-hearted and ready-witted. What better can we say of most of our friends?*

Lady Violet Greville, 'Men-servants in England', *The National Review*, February 1892

Loyalty existed on both sides. The notoriously demanding Lord Curzon was strangely tolerant of his dipsomaniac valet: the valet attended the Lausanne Conference, but he became overly 'tired and emotional' at a ball at Ouchy and disappeared, taking with him all his master's trousers – Lord Curzon forgave him.

## Valet's perks

A decent valet could rely on presents from visitors. While working for Lord and Lady Astor, Gordon Grimmett recalled how he became adept at acquiring clothes from visitors. Having received a handful of immaculate ties from Lady Astor's brother-in-law, Mr Lee the butler confirmed that he could keep odd garments donated by guests, and he began to build up a natty wardrobe. In time he also started to collect items 'left behind' by male guests, whose suitcases he had packed. Gordon's growing wardrobe nearly ended his career prematurely. He noticed that one of 'his' gentlemen, Mr Billie Astor, always wore his beautifully made shirts, underpants and vest only for one day. As Mr Billie also bathed twice a day, Gordon would retrieve these garments and wear them himself for a few days before putting them in the wash. He nearly met his nemesis in the formidable figure of Nanny Gibbons who waved a handful of dirty laundry at him and berated him for letting his master get so filthy. His narrow escape was timely – the following week one of the footmen was sacked for wearing a guest's cast-off socks.

Below: The travelling case used by Tommy Robartes in his bedroom at Lanhydrock, Cornwall. A gentleman's valet would ensure his master was equipped to face any eventuality while travelling.

# The footman

*He rises as late as possible, he exerts himself as little as he needs; he declines to take up the governess's supper or to clean her boots... several times a day he partakes freely of nourishing food, including a surprising quantity of beer... a jolly, magnificent fellow is the flunkey...*

Lady Violet Greville, 'Men-servants in England', *The National Review*, 1892

## The footman's reputation

In the nineteenth century, there was a general antipathy towards footmen, both on the part of employers, and their colleagues. Their masters resented paying the tax due on all menservants, but felt that no person of rank could be seen without footmen to serve at dinner. There was also friction with fellow servants; footmen were employed for their good looks and suave manners, and they were thought to be lazy and over-privileged.

In the eighteenth century, a dangerous age for wealthy travellers, footmen performed the function of bodyguards when their employers ventured out in a coach. They also accompanied the family on foreign trips, where they doubled as valets, general servants and occasionally as interpreters; a footman who could speak a foreign language was an asset when travelling overseas.

## The footman's appearance

'Matching' footmen were a preoccupation of the fashionable; in the same way that the rich might choose a pair of matching grey horses, footmen were selected for their physical similarity and aesthetic appeal. Height was a great asset, and tall footmen commanded higher salaries than short ones. At Cliveden the Astors' footmen were 6ft (1.8m) tall, and must have looked resplendent in a livery of striped red and yellow waistcoats under dark brown tailcoats.

## Livery

A footman's uniform was provided by the household, but occasionally thrifty masters would employ a new recruit who could fit into an existing set of clothes, as the outfit was expensive. Richard Scaddings, the most senior footman at Petworth until 1885, was paid £36 per annum, and his livery cost £32. Footmen's livery was based upon the fashions of the late eighteenth century, when gentlemen passed on their old clothes to their servants.

At Penrhyn Castle in the early 1900s, the footmen's day livery was blue tailcoats, black trousers and patent-leather boots, with white shirts, collars and narrow ties. In the evening, they wore navy-blue tailcoats with a bleeding-heart badge on the lapel, yellow waistcoats with black horizontal stripes, black plush knee breeches, black silk stockings and pumps. 'They didn't like this outfit very much,' recalled Annie Evans, former kitchen maid.

Perhaps the least attractive part of a footman's job was the need to powder his hair daily. Soap and water was carefully worked into the dry hair with a comb. White powder was then applied on top and would set rigid. The powder irritated the scalp, and had to be washed out at night, or else it could turn the footman's hair ginger in colour. There was a tax on hair powder until 1869, so some parsimonious householders insisted their staff use ordinary flour instead. Footmen embraced the use of horsehair wigs with relief; at least they could remove them at the end of each day.

# The footman's name

A new footman could expect a fancy set of clothes, even if 'previously worn', but he could also inherit his predecessor's first name. Many employers chose to call successive footmen by the same name. Lady Fetherstonhaugh of Uppark pronounced, 'I cannot understand why people make such a fuss what to call their footmen. I can call one "Enery" and the other "Hedward"...' By the early twentieth century 'Frederick' was the name commonly ascribed to the first footman in many country houses; the second would often be called 'Charles', regardless of his real name.

Above: A bill dated 1877 for livery bought from T.S. Freeman & Sons at Berrington Hall, Herefordshire.

Left: The livery of a footman, part of a set commissioned in 1904 by J.S. Tregoning of Landue, Cornwall, for his male servant at Lanhydrock.

# The duties of the footman

In the very grandest houses, where six or eight footmen might be on the staff, matching pairs of footmen often worked on a three-day rota. One day might be spent 'close waiting', in proximity to the master or mistress, serving meals and delivering messages. The next day would involve normal 'backstage' activities, such as cleaning silver or helping to valet one of the gentlemen. The third would be carriage duty. Bored footmen occasionally colluded with the coachman to create an impressive arrival at a fashionable address: after a sedate trot for most of the journey, the coachman would whip up the horses to a gallop for the last hundred yards, and as the coach careered to a halt, the footman would leap from the box and pound on the front door, before assisting his master or mistress sedately from their carriage.

Mrs Beeton, most of whose readership could only dream of employing liveried menservants, was dismissive of footmen:

*...when the lady of fashion chooses her footman without any other consideration than his height, shape, and tournure of his calf, it is not surprising that she should find a domestic who has no attachment for the family, who considers the figure he cuts behind her carriage, and the late hours he is compelled to keep, a full compensation for the wages he exacts, for the food he wastes, and for the perquisites he can lay his hands on.*

Isabella Beeton, *Mrs Beeton's Book of Household Management*, 1861

## Cleaning duties

However, footmen were not purely ornamental: they spent a great deal of time immured in the basement, washing the finest china and glass or cleaning silver, which was inclined to tarnish where coal fires and gas lighting were used. The footman tackled the silver with his bare hands, first mixing a soft, red powder known as 'rouge' with ammonia. The paste was applied to the silver, and rubbed in hard. Blisters would form as a result of the friction and the caustic nature of the mixture, but in time the footmen developed 'plate hands', impervious to heat, and covered by white cotton gloves when serving at table. The main challenge was to remove scratches from the silver cutlery, a lengthy process that mostly relied on friction with hands, followed by a polish from a chamois leather.

The cleaning of mirrors fell to footmen, as did the vigorous polishing of wooden furniture in the drawing room. Most footmen also spent a large part of the day cleaning paraffin lamps, as the

fumes from Colza oil left a smoky residue on the glass chimney or globe. In addition, until the universal adoption of electric light, many houses relied upon candlepower to supplement their gas or lamp light, to read a book, or to illuminate a darkened corridor in order to get to bed. Formal dinners remained candlelit even in houses where there was electricity; canny hostesses were aware that the soft glow of flickering candles was more 'forgiving'. Every morning, the footmen collected used candlesticks and candelabras from all over the house, and replenished the stocks. As one of their perks, footmen could sell the candle-ends to rag-and-bone dealers. They also assisted in maintaining the various woollen clothes used by male family members and senior servants. Suits, coats, cloaks and uniforms needed careful maintenance in an era before dry-cleaning. Lightly stained garments were carefully washed, dried, then suspended from a line and beaten with a cane to loosen the dirt, followed by vigorous brushing. In the better sort of house, the footman would have the use of a brushing room for all these functions. Here, tables, clothes horses and irons were readily available, as were ample hot and cold water.

Above: The Brushing Room, at Penrhyn Castle, Wales, in which all woollen clothes were brushed to keep them clean. Two top hats and a pair of boots await attention.

## Recruiting footmen

Although they spent much of their time hurrying up and down stairs, the footmen had the advantage over many of the staff: they did actually see the master and mistress and their visitors, and they managed to leave the house on a regular basis as part of their duties. However, their pay was modest – between £15 and £30 per annum.

Throughout the nineteenth and twentieth centuries, the number of menservants declined as women fulfilled some of their roles. Footmen were gradually replaced by parlourmaids; females were considered more reliable, their wages were cheaper than their male counterparts, and employers were increasingly reluctant to pay the tax imposed on male servants from 1777 until 1937. But there were households that continued to employ footmen for the sake of the dash that they cut; at Buckland Abbey in Devon, Sir Francis George Augustus Fuller-Elliott-Drake and Lady Elizabeth still employed liveried footmen in the first years of the twentieth century.

## The footman and the motor car

Perhaps surprisingly, the footmen's role of 'attending on excursions' survived the coming of the motor car. In the Edwardian era, a footman might accompany his master or mistress on trips by car, sitting next to the chauffeur as he had once sat alongside or behind the coachman, ready to assist his employers out of the car and to run errands at their destination. But the Great War cut a swathe through the ranks of both chauffeurs and footmen; in the first months of the conflict, employers were pressured to encourage their able-bodied menservants to enlist, and the resulting carnage was terrible.

Below: Morris Ten-Four car at Dunham Massey, Cheshire. The Morris Ten-Four was only in production from 1933 to 1935.

# The chauffeur

By the beginning of the twentieth century, the roll of servants at the grander houses included the chauffeur. Motoring was a rich man's hobby; the future Edward VII, who never stinted any expense on his own amusements, was an early enthusiast, taking his inaugural car ride in 1896 and buying his first vehicle in 1900.

The Prince's 'faster' friends were quick to follow, buying motor cars and employing liveried chauffeurs to convey them along dusty roads in conditions of some discomfort and danger. By 1904 there were 8,500 motor cars on the roads of Britain; owning a car was a tangible demonstration of the freedom that only serious wealth could buy.

Captain and Mrs Greville, friends of Edward VII, were early enthusiasts, acquiring a 12hp steam Serpolet in 1901, and two chauffeurs and a 'washer' to care for it. Smitten by the fashionable craze for 'motoring', Mrs Greville subsequently acquired one of the earliest models of Rolls-Royce, a Silver Ghost, in 1906, and later a Mercedes. Similarly, Rudyard Kipling was a pioneering motoring enthusiast; in 1911 he took delivery of a new Rolls-Royce. He wrote rhapsodically, 'A day in the car in an English county is a day in some fairy museum where all the exhibits are alive and real.'

Above: Chauffeurs and mechanics with Mrs Greville's fleet of cars in the stables at Polesden Lacey (1928).

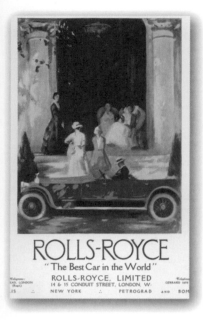

Above: Advertisement in *Colour* magazine (1917), for 'The Best Car in the World' – a Rolls-Royce convertible tourer.

Right: A Rover (c.1906), at Erddig, in Wales.

# French chauffeurs

The French noun 'chauffeur' means 'stoker' as the earliest experimental automobiles were often made in France and powered by steam. If one wanted to be driven, in the early years of motoring both hired man and newly purchased machine would be French in origin. The denizens of the servants' hall tended to be deeply suspicious of foreign terms, and new foreign colleagues; they were disparagingly known as 'shuvvers'. Careless of the rigid hierarchy that existed behind the green baize door, these interlopers rarely matched up to the butler's or head housekeeper's ideals of suitably deferential servant material, seeing themselves rather as dashing 'knights of the road', and often being unwilling to help in the house in any capacity. However, chauffeurs in their smart livery and more glamorous jobs were often popular with the female staff – George Archer, chauffeur at Lanhydrock, married one of the housemaids.

# Cars vs. horses

At many grand houses, cars were maintained alongside horses and carriages, with garages close to stable blocks for a number of years and an uneasy truce existed between the coachmen, grooms and stable lads and the 'rude mechanicals'. In Vita Sackville-West's novel *The Edwardians* (1930), there is an account of the elderly head carpenter's horror that his son, instead of following him into estate work, wants to go into 'the motor trade', as it's 'the coming thing'. Among the servant classes, it is significant – and perhaps rather poignant – that coachmen and grooms were often deeply resistant to retraining as chauffeurs, even when the growth of the native car industry allowed new opportunities for them to learn. The coachman at Lyme Park was trained to be a chauffeur, just before the start of the Great War, but this was unusual. Instead, most British chauffeurs tended to be drawn from the artisan class; skilled mechanics lured away from the new car factories, rather than steeped in generations of domestic service. Consequently they vigorously resisted any attempts to coerce them into helping the other staff by digging the garden or polishing the boots, as other male servants were expected to do when free of their usual responsibilities. *The Chauffeur*, an illustrated weekly magazine established in 1907, regularly debated whether the chauffeur was a servant or a professional, and (perhaps unsurprisingly) decided that he deserved respect and status for his skill as a mechanic, his resourcefulness and self-reliance, not to mention his enquiring, scientific mind. The editorial constantly sought to engender a sense of pride and patriotism within its readers.

## Early chauffeurs

Arthur Thompson became a groom at Polesden Lacey in 1907, when he was 17. He recalled the difference in status between himself and the chauffeur Charlie Smith: Arthur received 7/6d a week, but his friend Charlie received £1 a week, as well as accommodation and livery. Arthur recalled vividly how Charlie's successor, a German chauffeur called Hemmelkutz, was instantly dismissed by his employer, Mrs Greville, for coming to meet her in the wrong car:

*Hemmelkutz, he was quite nice, he was a German, but he was quite nice. She sacked him on the spot. She'd been abroad and she wrote to him to pick her up at Bookham Station with the Panhard at a certain time. He used to do all his repairs, and he'd got the Panhard laid out in the garage, all to pieces. So of course he didn't take the Panhard, he took the Mercedes. And when he came back he looked very down-in-the-mouth. 'Had some trouble?' 'Yes,' he said, 'I've got the sack. Yes, I took the Mercedes. She ordered the Panhard. "When I order the Panhard, I want the Panhard, not the Mercedes." … Yes, she sacked him, just like that. And he was a top man, he could get a job anywhere, just like that. They say she was very fair. Very hard though, I believe.'*

Some mistresses could be very tough. Mrs Venetia James, millionairess and doyenne of High Society, was so frugal that she allegedly had the Italian Ambassador, who had been a weekend guest at her country house, Coton in Cambridgeshire, returned to the station to catch the London train in the butcher's meat van, in order to save her chauffeur's petrol.

Others treated their chauffeur as a trusted servant. The Robartes family of Lanhydrock had been early supporters of the motor car. The family regularly motored between Cornwall and Cambridgeshire, and the heir Tommy Agar-Robartes was one of the first in the country to use the motor car for electioneering in 1906. The long-standing chauffeur was Henry Baker, and he drove Tommy's Rolls-Royce in France during the First World War, after it was shipped over in May 1915.

# The laundry maid

Clean laundry was a luxury in the nineteenth and early twentieth centuries; coal fires, candles, oil lamps and atmospheric pollution contributed to a great deal of household washing. Domestic laundry was labour-intensive and expensive; for middle-class families, sending the washing out, or employing a laundress for one day a week, was a significant part of the family budget. The very richest families could afford full-time laundry maids, women dedicated to caring for the household's textiles, such as napery and bedding, as well as its occupants' clothing. Only one in 266 domestic servants gave their occupation as laundry maid in the 1871 census.

Mrs Beeton, in her 1861 *Book of Household Management*, outlined the duties of the laundry maid, '…charged with the duty of washing and getting-up the family linen – a situation of great importance

where the washing is all done at home'. She advised the preparatory separation of the textiles according to their composition, and provided instructions on cleaning, washing, drying and ironing. In modest households, laundry day was usually Monday. In grander houses, with a fully fitted laundry and staff, the process was constant, except for Sundays.

On country estates, the laundry was usually well designed as a working environment, with sequential rooms. The washing house led into the drying room, then the ironing room. As it was heated by furnaces, the complex was usually independent of the main house to minimise the chance of fire.

At Dunham Massey, the laundry had been rebuilt in the 1720s and stayed in constant use until the early twentieth century. The head laundry maid in the 1870s was Janet Milligan from Dumfries; women from Ireland and Scotland were often in demand for their laundering skills, and were paid accordingly. Laundry maids' wages were about the same as those of the housemaids: between £12 and £30 per year.

## Laundry maids' morals

Laundry maids tended to 'live in' at country houses, but their morals were considered suspect, perhaps because they spent most of the working day unobserved by the housekeeper, and so had more opportunities to encounter male members of staff, such as gardeners and estate workers. At Castle Howard in Yorkshire, before the First World War, the laundry maids would clamber out of their quarters after dark, down ladders provided by the local lads, and sneak off to dances, returning the same way in the early hours. A more liberal attitude existed at Cheshire's Lyme Park, where three laundry maids shared a house on the estate.

## The duties of the laundry maid

Reporting to the housekeeper, the head laundry maid would collect and catalogue in her book the hundreds of individual items generated by a large household in the course of a week. These were separated and tackled according to their materials and degrees of dirtiness. In large houses the staff devised a coded laundry mark in indelible ink or in coloured stitching to identify each piece. A discreet inked mark of 'HB 3 42' was understood by the staff at Kingston Lacy to stand for 'Property of Henry Bankes [the master], one piece of a set of three, purchased in 1842'.

Left: Airing rack, mangle, wooden clothes horses, flat irons and other nineteenth-century laundry equipment at Ormesby Hall, Yorkshire.

### Soaking, washing and rinsing

Washing was done largely by hand, and the laundry maid pre-soaked the dirtiest items in tubs. Greasy cloths from the kitchen were steeped in unslaked lime and water, sometimes for days, before boiling. Laundresses used a number of devices to improve their results, from a 'dolly' to agitate the clothes, to a washboard.

Soap was sold by grocers in solid blocks; it was grated, then dissolved in hot water in a copper boiler to make a detergent solution. Lifting heavy baskets of wet washing and putting the clothes into very hot water containing washing soda, using large wooden tongs but without the protection of rubber gloves, was hard physical work in a hot and steamy atmosphere. The soaking, washing and rinsing process might take three days, to be followed by mangling, starching and drying. Sheets and towels were 'blued', given a slight tinge of Reckitt's Blue to make them appear whiter.

### Stain removal

There were many remedies to remove all sorts of stains. For example, boiling milk could lift the marks of spilt wine from linen or damask tablecloths and matching napkins, and there could be scores of them to wash after a weekend house party. Lemon juice was used on ink stains, salt was applied to port wine marks, and grease could reputedly be removed from silk by gently ironing the fabric over blotting paper. Handfuls of fresh ivy leaves were used for rinsing printed cottons. Boiled dark green ivy leaves also restored the depth of colour to faded black garments, a useful recipe in an era in which mourning clothes were worn so often.

### Delicate fabrics

Cottons and linens were robust enough to be laundered, but many textiles were difficult to clean. Brocades and velvets needed careful handling so as not to damage the texture, and natural dyes could be damaged if wrongly treated. In 1849 a Parisian tailor accidentally spilled some turpentine from a lamp on a tablecloth and discovered that it could remove stains. By the 1870s it was possible for garments to be dry-cleaned by posting them to a company called Pullars of Perth.

### The mangle

Mangling was the standard method of squeezing excess water from textiles. The most common design was the box mangle which measured 1.2 by 1.8m (4ft by 6ft), and was

Below: 'Ye Tudor' mangle, 1889.

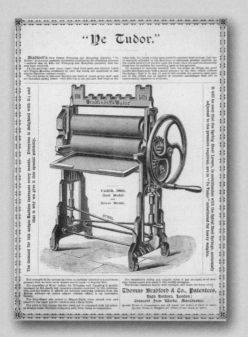

74

filled with stones to make it very heavy. Folded wet linen was wound around thick wooden rollers, the box was cranked over the fabric using a handle and the water was extruded. A box mangle was still in use at Shugborough in Staffordshire in the 1920s. It was so heavy to use that every Wednesday a handyman helped the laundresses operate it.

### Ironing and pressing

Where possible, damp linen would be laid out in the sunshine in order to bleach the fabric. Once dry, sheets and tablecloths were rolled up until it was time to iron them, which reduced the wrinkles. Starch made from potatoes or rice, or a proprietary brand, was used to give the ironing the required 'finish'. The irons were hefty to lift and troublesome to use; each was heated in succession on a special stove. The ironing board was a long low table, padded with calico-covered blankets. When frills and ruffles became fashionable, the resourceful laundry maid picked up her 'goffering tongs', similar to modern hair-curling tongs. It was source of pride for the laundry maids to turn out armloads of pristine, perfectly ironed napery.

The process of pressing fabric smooth with a heated iron was Chinese in origin and was uncommon in Europe until the sixteenth century. Flat irons remained the main method of ironing until the 1920s when electricity started to gain ground in the domestic setting. The preferred method of gauging the temperature was to pick up the iron and hold the flat side close to one's cheek; spitting on the surface, as portrayed so often in film and TV dramas, was definitely unacceptable.

Above: Flat irons and wooden clothes pegs in the Laundry at Wightwick Manor, Wolverhampton. Heated on stoves until hot, the irons were dangerous and ironing was a highly skilled job.

## Changing times

As the century ended, it became increasingly unusual for large households to employ their own laundry maids; at Knole the washing was sent out to the laundry in the village of Darenth. Few townhouses maintained their own laundries; there simply was not enough space. In addition, the level of air pollution was such that attempting to launder clothing in the city was futile. At some country houses, however, the whole process had always been done off-site: at Lanhydrock, the laundry was sent out to provide employment for the 'fallen women' of Bodmin and Loswithiel, as an act of charity.

# The governess

The governess in a well-heeled household was in an unenviable position; as a salaried employee, she was technically a servant, yet she was often shunned by the rest of the domestic staff because of her gentility and education. The governess did not belong to their class, yet she needed to work as they did, despite her social graces.

## The status of the governess

Governesses as educators of the young, especially girls, first appear in seventeenth-century accounts of British life; the Civil War and the plague left a large number of well-educated single women needing a role and the means to support themselves. Such women sought live-in posts in a large family, perhaps that of a distant relative, where they educated the daughters in return for their bed and board, and perhaps a small allowance. Charged with the moral welfare of the children, the status of the governess in aristocratic households was reasonably high.

Mary Ann Bullock, the former dairymaid who captured the heart of her master, needed schooling for her new role as Her Ladyship. The 18-year old was provided with a governess, Agnes Sutherland, who was about her own age and had been brought up in genteel circumstances nearby. After the marriage, Miss Sutherland became the new Lady Fetherstonhaugh's companion at Uppark in Sussex, an arrangement which suited all parties admirably.

## The governess in Victorian society

It was the growth of the moneyed classes and the subsequent enlargement of the number of servants they required that changed the view of the governess. By the time Queen Victoria came to the throne, women's parameters were focused on the home and hearth. Contact with the rough, tough world outside was not for ladies:

*...gentlemen may employ their hours of business in almost any degrading occupation and, if they but have the means of supporting a respectable establishment at home, may be gentlemen still; while, if a lady but touch any article, no matter how delicate, in the way of trade, she loses caste and ceases to be a lady.*

Mrs Sarah Ellis, *The Women of England*, 1839

A middle-class woman's place was in the home, a sanctuary for the paterfamilias after his busy day in the grubby world of industry and commerce. The popular image of Victoria and Albert, fecund and faithful, with a rapidly expanding nursery, exemplified the new view of a decent woman's aspirations. Paternalistic households expected their daughters to acquire decorative skills and a smattering of fashionable accomplishments suitable for snaring a wealthy husband. While their brothers went off to robust boarding schools, girls were kept cloistered at home and educated in a piecemeal fashion, by dancing instructors, French masters and, of course, governesses.

Above: *The Governess* (1844) by Richard Redgrave. One of the artist's sisters was forced to become a governess, an isolated position within the household.

## Distressed gentlewomen

For middle-class young women in straitened circumstances, becoming a governess was the only socially acceptable option. In previous centuries, women had worked as hairdressers, midwives, pharmacists or dressmakers, or had opened drapers' businesses or grocers' shops, without any loss of respectability, but now attitudes had changed. A well-brought-up young woman who needed money could not follow any trade. To become a governess was the least unattractive option for many of these 'distressed gentlewomen'.

### Finding a post

Governesses were expected to be well brought up – clergymen's daughters were particularly favoured. Informal networks and discreet enquiries through friends and their contacts were the preferred way of finding a post. Recruitment agencies were another route, though these often charged a commission. Only reluctantly did the prospective governess advertise in a local or national newspaper. *The Times* was the publication of choice; by the late 1840s, the paper carried advertisements for up to one hundred women a day seeking a post as a governess.

## Employing a governess

The Victorian family employing a governess would already have a cook, two housemaids, a nurse and a footman, according to Mrs Beeton, and an income of at least £1,000 (£43,160 today). However, the wages she could expect were often paltry: governesses between 1830 and 1890 earned between £35 and £80 (£1510 and £3450).

The wealthiest members of the middle classes copied the gentry's custom of employing governesses to educate their daughters. But modern mistresses seemed uncertain how to treat the governess, an insecurity shared by the other domestic staff. As Ursula Wyndham wrote in her memoir of Florence Court in County Fermanagh:

*[Governesses] were totally isolated. Parents left them in sole command of the schoolroom and treated them with the distant civility they extended to the domestic staff. The governess was intent on proving her gentility but nobody was interested. The servants were aware of the pretensions of she who presided in the schoolroom, and were in a strong position to put the governess in her place: she was, after all, just another paid employee.*

Ursula Wyndham, *Astride the Wall: A Memoir 1913–1945*, 1988

## Life as a governess

Tensions often ran high in the upper storeys of grander households when young charges were handed over to the ministrations of a new governess after years under the benign dictatorship of Nanny. Governesses also competed between themselves for the dominance of their charges. Lady Maud Baillie, born in 1896, recalled:

*There were two governesses, one French and one German, and not a word of English was allowed during meals. There was little co-operation between the two ladies, and, goaded by aggressive children, frequent Franco-Prussian wars took place.*

Neither servant nor lady, the governess often met hostility from the other domestic staff who resented any 'airs and graces'. The governess was expected to dress well on a very limited income and could not expect the perks that established servants enjoyed. However, to be a governess in an aristocratic home offered some advantages: the surroundings were attractive, she had access to a library and musical instruments, and there were excursions on which she acted as chaperone to her charges. Madame Orticia, the Robartes family's French governess at Lanhydrock accompanied the children all over the country for social functions and holidays, while Rosalie Chichester of Arlington Court and her family took her governess with them when they went on a Mediterranean cruise in 1877, so that the child did not miss her lessons while travelling.

Once her female charges had 'come out' into society, the governess might be asked to stay on, to act as chaperone and companion to the daughter until the girl's marriage, but usually she was dismissed with little more than the best wishes of the family, perhaps with a small pension. Occasionally, retired governesses might pool their resources and live together, opening a small day school to supplement their incomes. They feared ending up in the workhouse, because it would mark the final descent from any pretence of gentility, forcing them to exist alongside former servants, prostitutes or factory workers. Respectability was all; to become a pauper was seen as a terrible fate for a gentlewoman.

Below: The School Room at Lanhydrock in Cornwall, including the governess's desk, abacus, map and dresser with books and toys.

# The nanny and the nursemaid

Being a nurse or a nanny was a position of great trust and responsibility, caring for 'the heir and the spare'. Consequently, nursery staff were held in high esteem by both their employers and other servants. Nursemaids often stayed with a family for decades, eventually attaining the post of nanny, acting as surrogate mothers to the household.

In well-heeled families with small children, a nanny or nursemaid was an essential employee. With a high birthrate in the Victorian era, mothers employed competent females to change nappies, feed and care for their offspring 24 hours a day, and deal with frequent illnesses. In polite society, there was no alternative, and trustworthy children's nurses were highly prized. Families wanted the best care available, and competed to retain the services of reliable staff to take care of the next generation. As a result, by the 1890s, colleges such as Norland were providing professional training for young women keen to pursue this rewarding career.

*Other people's babies, that's my life*
*Mother to dozens and nobody's wife…*

Sir Alan Herbert, 'Other People's Babies', a song from *Streamline Revue*, 1934

## The wet nurse

The nursery of a grand house provided ample employment opportunities for various women involved in the care of young children. Wet nurses were young women who had recently had their own children, and so could breastfeed another woman's newborn baby; they would 'live in' until their services were no longer required. They were discouraged from drinking spirits, but the pragmatic Mrs Beeton advised they should have ample amounts of beer, stout and porter throughout the day, as breastfeeding mothers need large amounts of liquid, and beer was far safer to drink than water. Later in the Victorian era, with advanced medical knowledge, new mothers of all classes were encouraged to breastfeed their own infants, and were told they would regain their figures more rapidly by doing so. However, among the upper classes and the aristocracy, breastfeeding was generally still considered to be too 'animal' to be contemplated with anything other than revulsion.

## The duties of the nursemaid and nanny

Nursery staff were often recruited from large farming families, and began their careers early, leaving home at the age of 12 or 14 to take up a position as a nursery maid, waiting upon the more senior staff, cleaning, sewing and ironing. In time, a girl could be promoted to under-nurse and then to nursemaid, learning from her colleagues, and receiving between £20 and £25 (equivalent to £914 and £1,142 today) per annum. At a later stage she might find employment as the nanny of an important household, a figure of great authority.

Nurses and nannies formed strong attachments with their young charges from their earliest years, ministering to every aspect of the children's physical and emotional development. The child's relationship with its own parents was necessarily distant in aristocratic households; the old joke about a society lady only greeting her own child in the park because she recognised the nurse had some foundation in reality. Winston Churchill adored his nanny, Mrs Everest, who had been appointed to care for him within a month of his birth. They remained close throughout his adolescence, and exchanged newsy and affectionate letters while he was a schoolboy at Harrow. Though Winston loved his mother, he

Above: The Night Nursery on the second floor at Tyntesfield, Somerset. The children also had a playroom, called the Day Nursery.

saw so little of her that it was Nanny who was most important to him. In 1893, on the grounds of economy, and despite Winston's protests, Mrs Everest was dismissed and provided with a modest pension. Two years later, during her final illness he travelled from Sandhurst to see her, and to arrange and pay for a doctor. Elizabeth Everest's enthusiasm for the countryside of Kent was transmitted to young Winston and may have influenced his later decision to acquire Chartwell, with its unparalleled views of the Kentish Weald.

## The formidable nanny

Formidable nannies were much adored by their charges and their families. Nancy Astor described Nanny Gibbons, who started work at Cliveden in Buckinghamshire in 1907, as her 'strength and stay', much loved by the children. Sonia Keppel wrote of how her nanny's ritual of dressing in her uniform every morning fascinated her:

*Surprisingly, under her martial exterior, Nanny had a soft snail's body… the camouflage of her petticoat, concealing the pulling on of knickers; more whalebone, more starch, clamping down a vast bosom; the fastening of sharp buckles and a brooch, like the riveting of armour. With each controlling layer the pink folds were packed back into their shell until only I, as an eye-witness, knew of the vulnerability beneath her crustaceous façade…*

Sonia Keppel, *Edwardian Daughter*, 1958

## The status of nannies and nursemaids

Nursemaids tended to be local girls, whose relatives were also probably employed as servants elsewhere in the Big House, so the young recruit had allies outside the cloistered world of the nursery. As they spent nearly all their working days and nights caring for

their young charges, they tended to avoid the petty squabbles in the servants' hall. However they did have frequent contact with the master and mistress, who would either visit the nursery or have the children brought to them for a specified period every day. There were opportunities to complain directly to the householder at any infringement of their rights or shortfall on the part of other servants.

The nursery of any household was usually on the upper storeys, located at some distance from the adults' world. At Lanhydrock, the nursery wing is a complete suite of rooms, linked to the servants' bedrooms above and the kitchen below by the female servants' stairs. Almost like a self-contained apartment, it has a scullery, day and night nurseries, Nanny's bedroom, a bathroom and lavatory and a spare nursery or schoolroom. Each nursery had its own support staff of housemaids, and here Nanny reigned supreme. She dictated the layout and equipment needed, and insisted on amendments such as the installation of lockable bars on the windows or arrangements to lower the children out of the window in the event of a fire.

## Nursery life

During daylight hours, the inmates played in the day nursery; meals were delivered by the nursery maid or youngest footman. Nursery food was very dull: porridge, broth, steamed fish and minced chicken were the staples, and often it would return at every subsequent mealtime until it was consumed. Usually, Nanny would dine from a tray, though her elevated status entitled her to descend to 'Pug's Parlour', the housekeeper's room. The nursery staff were largely prohibited from fraternising with the other servants; their role was to provide constant protection for their charges. However, not all nurses were so diligent or scrupulous: occasionally small insomniac children were dosed with laudanum, containing morphine, or

Left: A print of a nursery frieze (c.1905), published by Lawrence and Jellicoe, at Lanhydrock in Cornwall.

Below: The Nursery Scullery at Lanhydrock.

gripe water, which contained alcohol. There were also some nannies who were cruel to their charges; in the enclosed world of the nursery, young children quickly learnt not to 'squeal'. Lord Curzon, later Viceroy of India, was terrified of his sadistic nanny, Miss Paraman, who beat her charges with slippers or brushes, and left them tied up in painful positions in the dark.

However, there were nannies who were adored by their charges and subsequently maintained an affectionate connection with 'their' family over the following decades. At Erddig, Lucy Hitchman became Nanny in 1903, and eight years later she married the Groom, Ernest Jones. Circumstances took them away, but in the 1940s they returned to Erddig as housekeeper and estate foreman. At Lanhydrock, the family treasured a head nurse, Mrs Tremlett, who had been employed shortly after the birth of Mary Vere Agar-Robartes and remained in 'esteemed' service for 25 years. Her sudden death in 1904 was reported in the *Cornish Guardian* with genuine regret and sorrow.

Below: The Day Nursery's collection of Victorian toys at Arlington Court, Devon.

Order and routine were the watchwords in the better-run nursery; children adhered to a strict timetable and lessons were alternated with periods of exercise and rest. Each activity required a change of clothing, and all children's clothes, including high-laced boots and outdoor wear, were kept in the nursery. The nanny had complete charge of the child's upbringing; indeed, most parents only saw their children for an hour or two each day, when their offspring were washed and changed, buffed and polished, and brought downstairs to be on their best behaviour. Strict hierarchy was rigidly observed from the outset in Nanny's treatment of the children. On expeditions to the park, the 'son and heir' was nearly always favoured over the other children and would be given over to Nanny's tender care, while junior siblings were in the care of mere nursemaids. Nannies also tended to refer to the juvenile heir by his rank when talking of him to the family or other servants.

Above: A stuffed pull-along elephant, one of many toys in the Nursery at Berrington Hall, Herefordshire.

Attractive nursemaids were particularly targeted by young men, their interest presumably piqued by the sight of a competent, domesticated female who was not only good with children, but, unlike other servants, was allowed out of the house to exercise her charges. *The Nursery Maid*, published in 1857, warned of the terrible fate that could await the naïve girl who allowed herself to be chatted up:

*A nursery maid is perhaps more exposed to danger than any other class of servant. She walks out a great deal with no other companions but children who are not old enough to know what is being said and whose presence affords a pretence and an excuse for addressing her. It is always dangerous to give ear to a man who is either too proud or too poor to marry you.*

No matter how close the bond between a nanny and her charges, the day would come when 'her' children left the nursery and were handed over to the daytime care of the governess. Where nannies were loved by their charges, the inevitable parting was traumatic. Both Sonia Keppel and Edith Sitwell were distraught when their beloved nannies were sent away, once the girls were deemed old enough to be schooled by a governess. It was a rare household in which a nanny and governess worked happily in tandem; Nanny held no brief for educated women who didn't fit into any of her known categories, neither servant nor mistress. Seething mutual resentment tended to exist between schoolroom and nursery, and children could become pawns in a battle of wills, though junior Machiavellis were often able to exploit the war of attrition for their own ends.

# 3 THE WORLD OF THE 'BIG HOUSE'

## The servants' quarters

Physical distance separated staff and employers. The family's realm was the ground (or upper ground) and first-floor level; the servants worked in the basement and ancillary buildings, and their sleeping quarters were under the roof. So divided were these two territories that the family almost never ventured into the working or living quarters of those they employed. The upper servants, the house steward or butler, and the housekeeper or cook, reported on personnel or logistical problems. Informally, the lady's maid

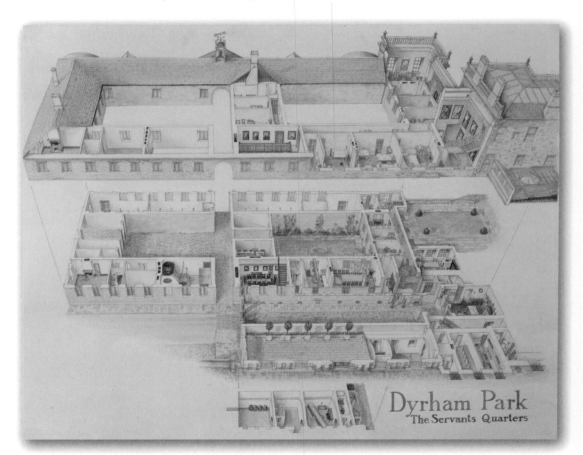

Dyrham Park
The Servants Quarters

or valet was likely to pass on selected gossip from below stairs, but the lower servants would have almost no contact with their employers.

*…the family constitute one community; the servants another. Whatever may be their mutual regard as dwellers under one roof, each class is entitled to shut its doors upon the other, and be alone… what passes on either side of the boundary shall be invisible and inaudible on the other.*

Robert Kerr, *The Gentleman's House*, 1864

## Staircases

A country house might have as many as six sets of stairs, to be used according to rank and purpose. In the servants' wings there would be separate men's and women's stairs; the main staircase was used by the family and their guests, the back staircase was the preserve of the servants. The bachelors' staircase allowed discreet access for restless visitors.

## Doors

The main front door was used by the family and their guests, and would be staffed at all times by the hall boy, overseen by the butler. At one side of the house there was usually a luggage entrance, where carriages would deposit cases, having dropped their owners at the front door. At Upton House the luggage lobby was also used by the family as an everyday entrance. But in fine weather the family and guests might use a garden entrance, while tenants and tradespeople would automatically come to the business entrance so as to reach the estate office. The kitchen complex was reached by the back door; this was where the head gardener would receive his daily instructions from the cook and where supplies would be delivered by the gardeners or delivery boys to be allocated to various storerooms.

## Townhouses

The issue of access was more complex in towns, the house being more at risk from opportunistic crime. The butler or head footman supervised the front door; lower orders were firmly directed to the tradesmen's entrance, usually in the 'area', down a flight of external steps at the front of the house. In cities, space was at a premium and consequently the servants' quarters needed to be compact. Kitchens and servants' halls were tucked away in basements or at the back of the house, and service stairs were essential to allow the staff discreet access to all floors. Servants' bedrooms were squeezed in under the roof, though the butler and cook maintained bedrooms near their own domain in the lower storeys.

Left: The servants' quarters at Dyrham Park, near Bath.

# Servants' bedrooms

Servants' bedrooms varied enormously, according to status and the attitude of the employer. Some were forced to sleep in what were little more than box rooms, full of lumber, without heating or adequate light. In more modest establishments servants might be expected to sleep where they worked. Thomas and Jane Carlyle moved into their house in Chelsea in 1834, and until they had a small servants' bedroom built in the attic in 1865, they expected their single servant to sleep either in the kitchen or in the scullery, though the Carlyles themselves each occupied a separate bedroom.

*A servant's bedroom should have as few articles in it as are consistent with comfort... The less carpet laid on the floor ...the healthier and freer of dirt it will be.*

Cassell's Household Guide, 1880

## Sleeping arrangements

In larger houses, menservants' rooms were completely segregated from those occupied by female servants, accessible only by separate sets of stairs, and a summary dismissal could be handed out to a servant found on the 'wrong' staircase. The standard layout consisted of a rather utilitarian corridor, often painted blue as this colour was believed to deter flies, running along the length of the house, just below the level of the roof; plain deal doors led off the corridor to individual servants' rooms. In earlier times at Stourhead maids had to share. In 1742 their 'Garrett' had a little table, three old chairs, five beds, three bedsteads, four bolsters, five blankets and four rugs. By the early 1900s, however, maids slept no more than two to a room.

Some domestic servants 'lived out', but this was unusual. An undated letter was carefully penned by Henri the sculleryman at Petworth to 'Monsieur', the French chef. Henri explained that he had been working in the kitchens at Petworth for six months, but was obliged to take lodgings in the town, rather than living in servants' accommodation on site, because he was married. He complained that he was paying a great deal of money for two small rooms. Might it not be possible, he asked Monsieur, for him and his wife to rent a cottage belonging to Lord Leconfield, just two or three rooms, with a small garden? Henri pointed out dolefully that this cottage would need to be close to Petworth House, '....because you know that in the kitchen, especially in the scullery, I am needed at all times, and if I were to live too far away, no-one would be able to come and get me if I were suddenly needed...'

## Furniture and fittings

Because of their location in the attics, servants' rooms were hot and stuffy in summer, and extremely cold in winter. Before the advent of reliable hot-water bottles, enterprising kitchen servants would warm a large saucepan full of sand on the range, and then divide the contents between a number of stout canvas bags, each secured with a drawstring, which they would put between the sheets to warm the bed before retiring. Being under the eaves, each room usually had a sloping ceiling and a small window, covered with a skimpy curtain. The walls were often painted white with distemper, though by the end of the nineteenth century 'servants' papers' were available from some commercial wallpaper manufacturers. Simple brass and iron bedsteads were standard, and while the rooms were rarely large they were at least private – for young people going into service, after growing up in a congested household, it was liberating to have their own bed, even their own room.

The furniture was usually of pine, sometimes painted in the family colours, and typically consisted of a washstand, a wardrobe and perhaps an armchair. Stripped wooden floorboards might be covered with a piece of carpet discarded by the family, or perhaps a home-made rag rug. A wind-up alarm clock might be provided by the housekeeper to ensure punctuality. Most maids arrived with a tin trunk with a domed lid, low enough to slide under the bed, to house their meagre belongings. A maid's or manservant's room often had an improving line of text or a religious maxim framed on the walls.

Below: The Fire Attic at Erddig, Wrexham, Wales, with a four-poster servant's bed. The bed has a sloping canopy, which was designed to fit under the eaves.

Under the enlightened Gibbs family of Tyntesfield, resident servants were very well treated. The men were housed above the servants' hall in a number of well-lit rooms, each one of which had its own fireplace. The female servants had similarly attractive and well-designed rooms on the second floor, above the kitchen.

### Lighting in servants' bedrooms

Servants had very little leisure and so spent little time in their bedrooms. Even here their lives were curtailed by regulations. They were allowed a lit candle to take to bed, but were under strict instructions not to sit up reading or, even worse, to read in bed. This was sensible, given the incidence of house fires caused by candles, but even when gas lighting came in it was rarely installed in the servants' bedrooms as the inmates might use it for their own pursuits. Writing in 1909, Borlase Matthews expressed the householder's dilemma – improved safety for the entire household versus ill-disciplined usage.

*The lighting of servants' bedrooms is a debatable point, as it encourages reading there, and consequent long hour burning… Still, the fire risk is greatly reduced if electric light is installed in these rooms and therefore it may be wiser to do so on this account. In some houses the lights in the servants bedrooms are so wired that they can be controlled by a switch in the dressing room or similar place, so that the consumer can extinguish their lights when he goes to bed himself.*

R. Borlase Matthews, *Electricity for Everyone*, 1909

To modern sensibilities, the imposition of instant darkness with a mere flick of a switch is reminiscent of prison life. However some saw the advantages of providing decent lighting: at Wimpole Hall in Cambridgeshire the servants' quarters were supplied with electricity before the rest of the house.

### Improved facilities?

At Red House, designed by Philip Webb for William Morris, the maids' bedrooms were in the rear wing of the house, with windows set high in the wall and at an angle, so that the inhabitants could see the sky, but not their surroundings. These rooms were so small that when a guest, Agnes Macdonald, was obliged to stay overnight in the housekeeper's room, she remarked 'I and my crinoline can't be contained in it.' This was little comfort for the housekeeper, forced to bed down for the night in an equally tiny room next door, already occupied by two housemaids.

Even in the bedrooms, the prevailing hierarchy was observed. The decoration of the rooms reflected the status of those who occupied them. Higher-ranking servants had comfortable, wallpapered rooms. While a scullery maid at Ickworth in Suffolk, Ida Ramsey, shared a room with a cold green linoleum floor; when she became second kitchen maid she was given a room of her own with a warm carpet.

While servants were essential to maintain the personal hygiene of the family in an era before piped water and flushing lavatories, they were ill-served themselves in the provision of bathroom facilities. Hot water had to be brought up to the room for washing, using the large jug and basin kept on the washstand, and removed after use; maids and menservants might be lucky enough to have a tin bath once a week, if the household was well-equipped. In the meantime, the lowlier servant had to make do with a 'stand-up' wash with a flannel and soap morning and evening. Domestic service manuals sternly reminded their readers of the need for personal hygiene, and insisted that servants pay particular attention to washing their feet, presumably because they recognised how much time was spent on them.

The chamber pot was kept under the bed, hence its slang name 'gazunder'. It would be the only recourse once the rest of the household was asleep, so it would need to be removed, emptied into an earth closet or water closet, cleaned in the sluice room with scalding water and returned to its discreet location every morning.

Left: Candleholder on a window sill at Hezlett House, County Londonderry, Northern Ireland.

Below: The Maids' Bedroom at Nunnington Hall, North Yorkshire.

## Servants' halls

By the middle of the seventeenth century servants tended to have their own dining room – previously they had all eaten with their employers in the great hall. The servants' hall functioned as a communal space in which the servants dined and socialised and where visiting servants were entertained. Here information was traded on news and events, and any limited free time was spent on hobbies or pastimes. Various activities were allowed in the servants' hall, once meals were over: sewing was popular, as the room tended to be well-lit, and cards were permitted in some places, though never on a Sunday. Some had a piano; and singing and dancing was allowed. Other occupations included reading newspapers and magazines, or studying, foreign languages being particularly popular. Writing letters home was a favourite occupation for many. Domestic service as a trade tended to be a family tradition, and successive siblings sent into service ended up all over the country. The Penny Post, introduced in 1840, allowed people on limited incomes to send a written message to any destination in the country for a flat fee. Incoming post was delivered to the butler's pantry and distributed every day by him.

### Furnishing of the servants' hall

The typical servants' hall tended to be a large ground-floor room with whitewashed walls and resilient, washable floors. Stevenson recommended:

*It should be plain, but comfortable; with a wood floor partly carpeted, rather than a stone one; furnished with a table for dining at, wooden benches and or chairs, and a cupboard or two. A fixed wash-hand-basin near it may be convenient… it is well to give it a pleasant outlook, but not over the lawn or garden, where the family may be sitting or amusing themselves. On the other hand, its inmates should not be overseen or overheard by the family. It should be close to the kitchen, for convenience in serving meals; not out of the way of supervision by the housekeeper; and near the back entrance, as it is used as a waiting room. When the men and women servants' apartments are on separate sides of the house, it forms the point of junction between them… servants [are] entitled to expect a reasonably comfortable sitting-room when their work is over…*

J.J. Stevenson, *House Architecture*, vol II, 1880

Servants' halls had their own cutlery, linen and china, often discarded items from 'upstairs', and their meals were cooked by one of the kitchen maids, gaining useful practice. In huge establishments, such as Petworth, there were under-servants, who only served other, more senior servants. At Ickworth, the system was like an apprenticeship; it was through serving their seniors that the younger servants learned to perfection tasks they would later be expected to perform for the family upstairs.

## Rules of conduct

Many servants' halls displayed a written list of rules regarding conduct and deportment. At Clandon Park the 'Rules to be Observed in this Hall' indicate how discipline was maintained in a communal space used by many different people. The system of forfeiture, or handing over a fine for transgressing one of the regulations, was common among many grand houses, but each set of rules seems to be specific to each house, presumably because of problems in the past. At Clandon, the rules hint at past friction between indoor servants and the grooms and coachman. As well as banning the cleaning of livery clothes or leather breeches at mealtimes, stable and other staff were required to keep their jackets on at dinner. In the Servants' Hall at Cotehele in Cornwall, apart from regulations insisting that hats be taken off once indoors (which hints at old battles about headgear), the main preoccupation seemed to be with time-keeping:

*Breakfast to be on Table by eight… Dinner to be on Table all the year by half past one O Clock & every person to appear clean & neat… Supper to be on Table by half past eight in Winter & nine O Clock in Summer & every Man belonging to the Hall to go to bed by ten in winter & half past ten in Summer unless ordered… or forfeit Sixpence.*

Printed rules hanging in the Servant's Quarters at Cotehele, c.1840

As the forum of 'below stairs' domestic life, it was important that the inhabitants of the servants' hall observed the regulations, as this contributed to greater efficiency and harmony.

*…Kitchen maids and scullery-maids eat in the kitchen. Chauffeurs, footmen, under-butler, pantry-boys, hall-boys, odd man, and steward's room footmen take their meals in the Servants' Hall, waited on by the hall-boy. The stillroom maids have breakfast and tea in the stillroom and dinner and supper in the Hall. The housemaids and nursery-maids have breakfast and tea in the house-maids' sitting-room and dinner and supper in the Hall. The head-housemaid ranks next to the head stillroom maid. The laundry-maids have a place of their own near the laundry, and the head laundry-maid ranks above the head housemaid. The Chef has his meals in a room of his own near the kitchen… Is there anything else I can tell you, Mr Marson?*

P.G. Wodehouse, *Something Fresh*, 1915

## Servants' meals

Rife with protocol, the thorny issue of meals in the servants' quarters of the grandest houses was a complete mystery to most outsiders. Who ate what, where and with whom was a reflection of the rigid hierarchy that survived 'downstairs' well into the twentieth century. Meals for the servants had to be scheduled so as to fit in with the 'upstairs' meals. Predominantly taken in the servants' hall in the basement, they could be intimidating affairs for the younger, lowlier or more timid members of staff. Fortunately, in many places the senior servants would either congregate in the steward's room, or retire after the main course to have their dessert in the housekeeper's room, allowing the junior staff a little more latitude.

### 'Dinner'

The midday meal was referred to as 'dinner' by the servants and was the main meal of the day; a hearty steak and kidney pie, or a roast of some sort, was followed by a weighty dessert, such as apple tart with custard. It was rare for servants to feel that they were underfed; in addition, there would often be leftovers sent back from 'upstairs', and these were consumed by the servants, who appreciated the better-quality food eaten by their employers. At Powis Castle in Wales in 1900, the kitchen maid 'C.M.B.' described the ritual:

*The Servants' Hall and Steward Room lunch was at 12:30pm. This had to be ready and on the Kitchen table three minutes to the half-hour. The Usher and Stewards Room footman would take it in. The Usher would then ring a bell and the maids who were lined up in the corridor would then troop in, and should one be a second late the door was shut and they got no meal…*

## Tea

Tea was also served in the servants' hall, usually after 'upstairs' had theirs, around 5.30pm. The butler, cook and housekeeper tended to take this meal in their own rooms. At Ickworth, the kitchen staff ate in the kitchen, at a small table in the corner, in order to monitor the food that was cooking. They generally had a large meal at about 5 o'clock, because they would be busy during the period before the family's dinner, when the other servants would be eating their supper. This was known as a 'meat tea', a more substantial version of the tea and cake enjoyed by the other servants in the afternoon.

After the dinner was served 'upstairs', at about 9pm the servants would have their supper 'downstairs', before clearing away and preparing for the next day's work.

Above: The Cook's Sitting Room with the table laid for tea at Penrhyn Castle, Gwynedd.

# The kitchen

The kitchen was the hub of domestic operations, and a hot, steamy and noisy working environment. In a large household, the kitchen staff were constantly occupied taking in and storing deliveries, preparing food, plating it up and dispatching it to various destinations. The key element in the kitchen was the clock; it needed to be synchronised with the family's clocks upstairs and the butler's fob watch, so that meals could be served on time.

## Cooking methods

Kitchens in big houses relied upon various methods of cooking to prepare meals. The oldest houses often still had a sort of a spit, where whole carcasses could be impaled on a metal rod and turned, cooking the meat in the heat of the flames from the fire below, and catching the dripping in a flat tray underneath. More advanced spits were turned by a fan set into the chimney and driven by the rising heat and smoke. A variant on this method was a clockwork device known as a roasting jack, which could be wound up by hand, allowing the meat to revolve gently above the heat; a large copper drip pan was placed underneath to catch the meat juices.

Below: The Open Range in the Kitchen at Petworth, Sussex. Parts date from the early nineteenth century.

A technological improvement on the open fire was the cooking range. A central open fire heated an oven on one side and a boiler on the other; this offered 'hobs', hot surfaces on which saucepans, pots and kettles could be used, as well as enclosed ovens for baking. Most houses had separate bread ovens and pastry ovens, allowing more control over the foodstuffs to be cooked inside them. Ranges were mostly fired with coal, which was stored nearby; at Osterley Park, Middlesex, the waist-high divisions within the extensive coal pens give an indication of the vast amount of fuel stored and expended on site. At Chirk Castle near Wrexham the massive open range consumed 5cwt (254kg) of coal a day.

The heat generated by cooking ranges mostly dispersed up the chimney, and by the 1840s manufacturers were improving their designs. 'Kitcheners', as they were known, were smaller and more adaptable; stews and stockpots could now gently simmer for hours on a 'backburner', while removing a circular lid exposed a saucepan to the heat source underneath, for quicker cooking. The food was less likely to become polluted with soot or cinders, and the kitchener also provided the hot water needed for bathing and washing.

Gauging the heat of any oven was a matter of experience and guesswork. In 1882, Mrs Black's *Household Cookery and Laundry Work* advised cooks that if a sheet of paper thrown into the oven caught fire, the oven was too hot; but if it turned dark brown, the oven was safe to use for cooking pastry. A light brown piece of paper indicated the temperature was suitable for pies, and light yellow would be fine for cakes. As Robert Kerr stated in *The Gentleman's House* in 1864, the Victorian kitchen had '…the character of a complicated laboratory…'

Solid fuel remained the normal heat source for running a range in country districts well into the twentieth century. Although piped gas was used for street lighting as early as the 1820s in London, the use of gas for cooking throughout the Victorian and Edwardian eras was confined largely to newly built middle and lower-middle class homes in the suburbs of big cities. A gas cooker could not supply the vast quantities of hot water produced by a solid-fuel range.

## 'Pestilential vapour'

The kitchen was often a very hot place in which to work. So in the Victorian era kitchens were designed to be double height, allowing the heat to rise to a lofty ceiling. The windows faced north or east, so as to keep them as cool as possible. Often the upper reaches of the kitchen walls were painted white or blue, a colour thought to deter flies. The whole complex needed to be easy to keep clean; the lower 1.2m (4ft) of so of walls was usually covered in ceramic tiles or glazed bricks, simple to wash down, and the floors were typically covered in flagstones, also easy to scrub.

Wooden duckboards sometimes helped to ease the aching feet of the cook and her staff, but contemporary accounts detail how kitchen staff, especially cooks, tended to suffer with their feet. Hardly surprising, given their intensive work schedule seven days a week and the fact that boots were rarely uniformly sized or shaped to fit left or right feet but were 'worn in' by their owner to give an approximation of comfortable footwear.

*…the kitchen, where the pots and range glisten in the light, where the cheery cook turns mountains into molehills and frugal fare into a feast…*

Architect Edwin Lutyens, in a letter to his fiancée, 1896

## Kitchen equipment

Essential kitchen equipment was displayed on shelves or wooden dressers, with extra open storage beneath tables and work surfaces, for immediate use. The copper *batterie de cuisine*, a huge assortment of pots, pans and moulds lined with a thin coating of tin, was displayed on view, and each item's sparkling appearance was taken to be a mark of honour. Mrs Hardy, the cook at Chirk Castle, would show potential kitchen maids the ranks of copper pans, and tell them she required all her cooking utensils to be '…like a new penny, every one of them, big or small, and the inside must look like a silver threepenny bit. Can you do that?' If the answer was in the affirmative, the candidate was given the job.

Central to the kitchen was a vast wooden table, the work surface used by the cook or chef and their kitchen maids. The table at Attingham Park was described in an inventory of 1827 as 'a capital stout elm-topped table, 16 feet x 4 feet 4 [5m x 1.5m]'. Every

Left: Part of the copper *batterie de cuisine* on the dresser shelves in the kitchen at Attingham Park, Shropshire.

morning, the kitchen maid would use a stiff scrubbing brush, a
solution of soda in hot water, and sand to clean the surface and legs
of the kitchen table. The legs of the table were often mounted on
blocks of stone so that water could not collect under the base and
rot the wood, a necessary precaution as the kitchen floor might be
washed or scrubbed three times a day.

## Kitchen design

Where an architect considered the business of cooking and designed
a kitchen and ancillary spaces, the result could be a treat for the eye
as well as a joy in which to work. At Castle Drogo in Devon, Edwin
Lutyens drew on his genuine passion for kitchens to create a
deceptively simple room, with natural light and ventilation from a
circular lantern above. At least two-thirds of this spacious kitchen
lies below ground level, counteracting the great heat given off by the
two black-leaded coal ranges, which were alight 24 hours a day. The
kitchen in Powis Castle, Powys, in 1900 was also a delight, according
to one kitchen maid, 'C.M.B.', who described it as:

*A lovely place in which to work, it was I think quite 30 feet [9m] long, one
whole side being taken up by the dresser, which had dozens and dozens of coppers
of all sizes reclining on its shelves. On the port board were big braziers, fish
kettles and stock pots and hanging on the partitions of the dresser were copper
mixing bowls. Under a very big window were the charcoal stoves. There were six
and built at intervals on a brick sort of slab. This would get very hot and keep
things boiling for hours. At the other end of the Kitchen the spits hung, four plain
ones and one cradle spit. These were cleaned with the same mixture as the inside
of the coppers, silver sand on which boiled soft soap had been added, and the
outside, silver sand, salt and hot vinegar.*

Kitchens often had a large serving hatch giving on to the servants'
corridor, through which table-ready dishes would be passed, a little
like modern restaurants today; at Lanhydrock big wooden trays
laden with food were passed to serving staff waiting in line on
the other side. The servants' corridor was often designed to have
a number of right-angled turns, as at Tyntesfield and perhaps with
a swing door halfway along – both devices were methods of keeping
smells from the gentry's living quarters on the floor above. In
addition, the 'boundary' separating upstairs and downstairs was
marked by a stout door covered with heavy green baize, marking
the divide but also absorbing the clamour and smells emanating
from the lower regions.

# From the kitchen to the dining room

In many country houses, the kitchen was located at some distance from the main body of the house. The distance from subterranean kitchen to dining room might be so large that it would have a deleterious effect on the food. At Uppark in Sussex, until 1895 when the kitchen was moved closer to the house, hot food was transported along underground passages on trolleys equipped with charcoal-heated hot-cupboards, and up the service staircase.

Transporting the food to the table required organisation, and nimble staff, who were able to carry laden trays up steep stairs. Usually a flat surface such as a butler's tray stand would be provided along the route so that the bearer could put the tray down for a moment to open the door into the dining room. Often the door would be cunningly disguised; at Osterley Park in Middlesex the service door in the corner of the dining room is almost imperceptible.

## Anterooms and folding screens

In some houses, such as Lanhydrock, an anteroom was provided next to the dining room. Here the butler supervised the arrangement of dishes, and marshalled the footmen so that each course could be served simultaneously. The footmen would be briefed as to which of the diners was their responsibility. Where no anteroom existed, a folding screen in the dining room often provided a useful hidey-hole for less scrupulous staff. Bacon, Mrs Greville's notorious butler at Polesden Lacey, was once glimpsed behind the screen, shovelling all the lambs' tongues from the plates he was about to serve into his mouth. The House Steward, Bole, protected his errant colleague by reporting that regrettably, the cook had been unable to acquire lambs' tongues after all, and with aplomb he served the mystified diners with gravy-stained but otherwise empty plates.

## The right temperature?

Astute hostesses were anxious to ensure that food and drink were served at the right temperature: the servery at Lanhydrock contained a heated steel hot-cupboard, fuelled by the central-heating system, so food arrived on the table piping hot. Correct storage for wines was also a priority for some: at Polesden Lacey an early refrigerator was installed so that white wines could be suitably chilled. However, not all hosts were so concerned with their guests' comfort: Benjamin Disraeli was once reported to have murmured gloomily, 'At last, something warm' as he was handed a glass of champagne at a country-house dinner.

Below: The servery at Lanhydrock. The food was kept warm in the great steel hot-cupboard. It was fuelled by the coal-fired central-heating system.

# Bathrooms and water closets

Baths were uncommon at the beginning of the nineteenth century in Britain. The technology to heat water and pump it through a domestic system was available by the 1840s, but the vast majority of the population preferred to avoid the disruption and expense of introducing pipes and boilers and cisterns, especially when servants could provide a modicum of reasonably hot water. Besides, how clean was clean? The master of one Cambridge College refused to countenance the introduction of baths for the students on the grounds that the undergraduates were only resident for eight weeks at a time. Queen Victoria, on her accession in 1837, discovered that Buckingham Palace had no bathroom and used her personal allowance to have hot water piped into her bedroom so she could have a bath.

## Managing personal hygiene

Most people with any pretensions to gentility relied on vigorous washing of the parts of the body that showed, such as hands, face and neck, and strip-washing to reach the parts that didn't. Ablutions took place in the privacy of one's bedroom or dressing-room, using a large basin and a jug of warm water placed on a birchwood washstand – birchwood resisted water staining.
Standing on a linen towel, the bather applied warm water and soap with a wash cloth or sponge, then rinsed off the residue. A sponge bath required a wide, shallow pan full of warm water in which the person stood to wash and rinse themselves; the more determined would order a tub in which they would sit in warm water. Having a bath required preparations: the floor needed to be covered with a waterproof oilcloth, the fire stoked up, and the portable tub brought in and filled by servants bearing hot water in brass jugs. Folding screens reduced draughts, and after completing his or her ablutions, the bather would be wrapped in thick towels, and urged to rest.

In the newly industrialised cities, it was apparent that virulent epidemics originated in dirty, overcrowded neighbourhoods. City authorities were galvanised into action, to tackle the slums

Below: The Dressing Room at Carlyle's House, London, the home of writer Thomas Carlyle and his wife from 1834 to 1881. The hip bath shown would have been filled using jugs of water and was designed to be sat in.

by improving the hygiene of the slum-dwellers. The poorer classes were less able to keep themselves clean in the first place. One method of distinguishing oneself as being socially superior was to be cleaner and more fragrant. By the time that William Thackeray came up with the term 'the Great Unwashed' in his novel *Pendennis* in 1849, being clean had become a signifier of class.

## The emergence of the bathroom

With the arrival of piped water and the development of the water-heating boiler, the bathroom developed as a separate, single-purpose room in the modern Victorian home. Wealthy householders employed plumbers and engineers to introduce magnificent facilities; baths of all shapes and sizes, with decorated ceramics for the lavish, cast iron for the more spartan. Early encounters with sanitaryware were not always successful: the fictional Mr Pooter (of George and Weedon Grossmith's *Diary of a Nobody*, 1892) painted the inside of his bath with red enamel, only to have the substance transfer itself to his own extremities when he ran the hot tap.

## The bath

Baths gained the upper hand among the more affluent middle classes in cities. There were some misguided attempts to heat bathwater *in situ* and to maintain its temperature without the intervention of servants. In 1851 William Tyler invented a bath that was heated from underneath by burning coal. The following year John Everett Millais, the Pre-Raphaelite artist, spent days painting model Lizzie Siddal posing as Ophelia fully dressed, lying in a weed-strewn bath, which was heated 'by lamps underneath'. Perhaps unsurprisingly, she contracted pneumonia and the painter was forced by her father to pay her medical bills.

## Showers

Showers needed only a small water supply and the earliest patent for a shower dates from 1767; by the time of the Great Exhibition in 1851, numerous designs were available. They either required hand-pumping, for solo operation, or the co-operation of a servant; but until the coming of designated bathrooms with adequate drainage, and ample supplies of warm water provided by a mechanical pump, showering was seen as a somewhat eccentric method of keeping clean in chilly Britain.

## Country-house plumbing

Some households embraced the new technology with a vengeance: at Cragside in Northumberland, the house was designed with a whole

DOMESTIC SANITARY REGULATIONS.

suite of bathrooms, a plunge bath, and a large 'hammam' or Turkish bath, covered in beautiful blue tiles. Despite its venerable, High Gothic appearance, Tyntesfield in Somerset was at the cutting edge of technology when it came to plumbing: there were independent bathrooms, a dedicated shower room in one wing, and numerous water closets; there were even two WCs for servants, an enlightened arrangement for the 1860s.

But country houses were slow to adopt the new-fangled methods of bathing. Partly this was for practical reasons: inserting a decent plumbing system in a rambling and idiosyncratic old building was often a daunting engineering prospect. There was also antipathy for the modern, self-operated, functional, designated bathroom – it was seen as *nouveau riche*. Even at Lanhydrock, largely rebuilt in the 1880s, only two bathrooms were installed, one for the family and one for the children. The 1886 inventory suggests the continued use of hipbaths. Indeed, few large houses had more than one or two bathrooms until the end of the nineteenth century.

At Felbrigg Hall in Norfolk in 1861, Agnes Willoughby, who was marrying the eccentric heir 'Mad' Windham for his money, insisted as a condition of her marriage that an enamel bath with hot and cold

Above: *Domestic Sanitary Regulations*, a cartoon (c.1851), printed in *Punch*.

Above: The
washstand in
Miss Rosalie
Chichester's
Bedroom with
a ceramic bowl
and ewer, soap
dish and matching
candlesticks,
at Arlington
Court, Devon.

running water was installed for her. Her fiancé refused; the marriage
went ahead, but was short-lived. Agnes bolted with an Italian singer,
presumably for warmer climes and lavish supplies of constant hot
water. 'Mad' Windham 'remained faithful to the hipbath all his
days', and a plumbed-in bathroom was only introduced in the
1920s, six decades too late for Agnes.

Even some forward-thinking architects believed that servants
could compensate for a lack of bathrooms: at Lindisfarne Castle,
Northumberland, there were nine bedrooms but only one bathroom;
guests were provided with jugs of hot water for their hipbaths in
front of log fires in their bedrooms, and nightstands contained
chamber pots. A second bathroom was installed much later, but
the facilities were still less than convenient for staff and guests.

Bathing in a portable bath could never have been ideal. Splashing
generated a great deal of extra water to be cleaned up. As Mrs
George Fraser remarked in her prescient book *First Aid to the
Servantless* in 1913, a gentleman should show some consideration
in his bathing etiquette: 'He need not splash in his bath tub like
a hippopotamus at the Zoo', and he should put away his own
clothes afterwards. Interestingly, even where country-house
owners started to install bathrooms, female guests were reluctant
to leave the privacy of their bedroom at the risk of being seen 'at
a disadvantage', either in one's state of dress or on one's way to
undertake a necessary bodily function. In short, if a room did not
have *en suite* facilities then the occupier would almost certainly
request a portable bath. Lady Fry summed up prevailing attitudes
by saying sniffily that bathrooms 'were only for servants'.

# Lavatories

At a magnificent evening reception in London, the newly married Lady Lavery queued to have her arrival announced by the major-domo. Shyly, she mumbled her somewhat unfamiliar name in his ear, but instead of pronouncing it resonantly to the assembled masses, he turned to her and whispered, 'Back down the stairs, Ma'am, the door to the left is the cloakroom…'.

The question of bodily functions, and how to accommodate them, had exercised the minds of the polite and impolite for centuries. Any dwelling with a patch of land outside had an 'outhouse' or 'privy', essentially a wooden shed containing a latrine in the form of a pit, topped with a wooden bench with a hole in it to form the seat. In time, the pit would be filled in with topsoil, another hole dug nearby, and the hut would be relocated to cover it. In Wales, the structure was known as '*Ty bach*', the little house. Where facilities were located indoors, other euphemisms applied; visitors asked for 'the smallest room', while the term the 'closet' was used to mean a closed room, somewhere providing some privacy. Often, in aristocratic houses, it was the place where one could use the 'closed stool', a chair-shaped structure rather like a modern commode, with a removable pewter pan. In time it became known as the 'lavatory', meaning the place where one washes, and then the toilet, meaning the act of washing. Closets were of two types: the users of the earth closet outside the house covered anything deposited in it with a layer of fresh soil, but the bucket had to be emptied sooner or later – in cities this thankless task was executed by 'night soil men'. In the country, it was part of outdoor servants' duties. In the water closet, a supply of water washed away any detritus into a complex system of plumbing, which either found its way to a cesspit, or in cities eventually joined a sewer.

## The chamber pot

For indoor use, chamber pots continued to be used in all classes of British households well into the twentieth century, especially in places where alternative facilities were located out-of-doors or many floors away. At Penrhyn Castle, the dining room was far from the 'necessary offices' and so at one end of the dado a cupboard was built to conceal Burleigh chamber pots, ceramic pots for use by the gentlemen, after the ladies and the servants had withdrawn (see page 106). Socially adept ladies might similarly take this opportunity to ask their hostesses discreetly if they could 'retire' for a moment, and would be directed to a spare room, complete with folding screen and prominently placed chinaware.

Above: Outside lavatory in the Courtyard of Court 15, Birmingham Back to Backs. This is an 'earth closet' with no mains sewage pipe, just a bucket which would have been emptied and the contents collected weekly by the 'night soil men'.

Right: The carved wooden dado in the Dining Room at Penrhyn Castle conceals a cupboard that held a chamber pot for the relief of gentlemen diners.

In grander establishments, it was considered normal for the servants to remove, clean and replace chamber pots from every bedroom four times a day. These receptacles were either left under the bed, often with a lid on, or stored discreetly in a 'night cupboard', which looked like a bedside table but would, understandably, be located at some distance from the bed. In the better-equipped houses, the housemaid's cupboard on the upper floors had two sinks, into one of which chamber pots were emptied, and the sink next to it was used for the washing of 'bedroom ware' with hot water and soda.

Because of their shape and inevitable rough treatment, chamber pots were prone to accidental breakages and housekeepers were recommended to invest in a large stock of identical models for replacements. Servants were also supplied with chamber pots to be used in their bedrooms – these were normally plain white.

## The WC

Despite the ubiquitous use of chamber pots there must have been a certain amount of mutual embarrassment. Consequently, the water closet was seen by many as a sign of progress and enlightenment. The 'WC' was showcased at the Great Exhibition of 1851 where public facilities were provided for the visitors at a penny per visit. However, only 14 per cent of the Great Exhibition visitors used the WCs; the other 86 per cent showed great powers of endurance.

Scottish architect J.J. Stevenson recommended that such facilities should also be introduced for servants:

*In every house which pretends to convenience and perfection in planning, there must be several water-closets – in no case fewer than three – for the male and female portions of the family, and for the servants... That for the servants is more conveniently placed down-stairs than beside their bedrooms, but large houses may have one in both situations, and they should have separate ones for male and female servants.*

J.J. Stevenson, *House Architecture*, vol. II, 1880

## Facilities at Red House

Red House in Bexleyheath was designed to look timeless. However both architect and client were willing to embrace new technology if it suited their requirements. A fully flushing water closet was installed on the first floor for the ladies, and another on the ground floor for gentlemen. In an outhouse in the yard was a privy for the servants, which was 'flushed' using buckets of water. Interestingly, there was no plumbed-in bath. In re-creating his vision of the Middle Ages, William Morris favoured bathing in front of a roaring fire in one's own bedroom, in a portable tub supplied with copious amounts of hot water provided by discreet servants. Morris may have been a principled philanthropist and an important Socialist ideologue, but he was also a moneyed Victorian gentleman who relied upon compliant domestic staff to minister to his needs.

## Sanitary improvements

Clean paper of all types was saved by the household and used as lavatory paper, before the commercial production of this commodity. Assorted paper squares would have a string threaded through one corner and the pad would be hung in each lavatory. Making up pads of loo paper was one of the many tasks routinely given to housemaids. Manufacturers recognised the potential of this market but it wasn't until 1879 that perforated, commercially produced lavatory paper was available in Britain. By 1907, the Army and Navy Stores catalogue offered 'Mikado' soft toilet tissue by post. 'British No. 1 Thin', later known as Bromo lavatory paper, was first marketed in 1890 and continued in production until 1989.

The arrival of reliable indoor plumbing, the provision of instant hot water from the tap and the indoor WC removed at a stroke a large part of the housemaid's burden. Cleaning the WCs every day was no hardship by comparison to emptying the chamber pots of one's superiors, and housemaids were liberated from some of the less appealing aspects of their daily drudgery.

Below: Advertisement for a toilet paper holder (1894).

BEAUTIFULLY BRONZED,
and Fitted with:
A ROLL OF TOILET PAPER,
67 yards long, containing
384 squares, and adjustable
clip for refilling;
A BOX
for
MATCHES,
with Striker;
A
BRACKET,
with Socket
for
LAMP
or
CANDLE;
A SILVERED BEVELLED
MIRROR;
A RECEPTACLE FOR
TOBACCO ASH,
CIGAR AND CIGARETTE ENDS;
AND
TOWEL HOOK.

SIZES, 16 INCHES BY 10 INCHES.

Price **5/6**, Complete as drawn.
If without Lamp, and with Plain Mirror, **4s. 6d.**
Can be supplied with our special "ELEKTRON" finish, 1s. 6d. extra.

# The spring clean

The nineteenth and early twentieth centuries were an astonishingly filthy era, especially for those living in cities. Coal dust was all-pervasive; it left a gritty residue, a black and sticky coating of soot. Gas lighting gave off fumes that tarnished silver and brass, and candles smelt, smoked and dropped gobbets of hot wax. Effective detergents were still in their infancy, and maids waged a war against 'smuts' on every surface.

## Major cleaning

A programme of cleaning and repairs was undertaken once or twice a year, usually when 'the family' were away, perhaps travelling on the Continent, or doing the London Season, with their senior servants. The other servants remained at the country house, under the direction of the housekeeper.

Spring cleaning began in April or May, after the chimneys had been swept. The house staff received extra payments, which enabled them to make their own arrangements for food and beer. Often they pooled their allowances, nominating the most able kitchen maid to be their temporary cook, and each would contribute the same amount every day for communal provisions. Any money left over was split equally between the participants.

Below: Foamo washing powder advert (c.1900).

### Chimneys first

It made sense to tackle the dirtiest jobs first, so the chimney sweep tackled the chimneys. At Stourhead in 1863, Sir Henry Hoare issued detailed, printed instructions to the household staff, insisting that 'All these Chimneys should be Climbed, as some of the Chimneys are too large for the Sweep's broom, and others are very crooked…' To comply, the sweep would send the smallest and nimblest of his employees up the chimneys to dislodge the worst of the soot. Using children for this purpose had been banned in 1840, but the practice continued surreptitiously and the law against it had to be reinforced in 1864.

## The top floors

Preparation was key to the house-cleaning process: furniture was moved away from walls before being polished, to avoid possible damage to wall-coverings; precious pieces would be wrapped in protective 'case covers', many of them purpose-made from cotton for that particular chair or table; chamois leather 'stockings' were fitted to gilt furniture, and leather covers placed over pianos. Dustsheets protected other fittings and fixtures.

If the weather allowed, windows were opened and heavy curtains taken down and shaken to remove the accumulated dust, before being brushed and dabbed with wet sponges. Paintwork was washed, as were the windows. Flock wallpaper was tackled with handbellows, to blow off the dust; soft brushes were used on the intricate carvings on picture and mirrors frames. The chandeliers and pier glasses were cleaned with cloths or sponges dampened with water or spirits of wine, then dried and buffed.

## Floors

Floors were treated with great care; carpets were rolled up, carried outdoors and beaten and swept by the staff. Harry Jackson of Lyme Park described the effort required: 'We would take all the carpets up and take them up on Cage Hill in a pony cart and beat them. There'd be twenty odd fellows up there, beating, brushing, sweeping the carpet.' After cleaning, carpets could be rolled and stored until just before the family's return, to save them from wear and tear and the effects of sunlight. While the carpets were drying, the floors underneath were treated: wooden floors were scrubbed, paintwork wiped down with a solution of vinegar in warm water and polished with a wash-leather (a chamois leather). Grates were thoroughly black-leaded and burnished to a high shine, and mutton fat was used on slate hearth stones for a glossy finish.

# Home-made cleaning materials

Many housekeepers made their own recipes for cleaning materials.
In Mrs Hale Parker's handwritten *Book of Receipts* of 1876 there
are recipes for household products: blending a teacupful of spirit
of wine and some black sealing wax 'Makes good varnish', states
the succinct comment underneath. 'To clean marble', she continued,
slightly ungrammatically, 'Mix and to be powdered [sic] very fine
2 oz common soda, 1 oz powdered pumice stone and 1 oz chalk.'

All wooden furniture was buffed with a home-made mixture
of beeswax and turpentine; all ornaments carefully washed and
replaced. Tapestries and upholstery were brushed and stains
spot-treated with benzene, an early form of dry-cleaning. The
housekeeper would take stock of the household linen, relegating
shabbier items to the servants' linen store. Cupboards and chests
of drawers were turned out and checked for signs of moth or insect
infestation. The housekeeper would also direct the maids to check all
the china and glass used by both the family and the staff; cracked or
damaged items would be discarded, and requests for replacements
sent to department stores.

# Maintenance projects

Any large maintenance or improvement project was also tackled
while the family was absent: a new range might be brought in, the
plumbing and drainage might be improved, or electricity could be

installed. The disruption caused by technological innovations was immense, as recalled tongue-in-cheek by the London sophisticate Mlle. Sans-Gêne' (or 'Mlle. Shameless'):

*Monday: my mother has said, let there be light, and there is not a glimmer, and the electricians are still busy doing nothing. The gas has been cut off pending their operations; the quality of the grocer's candles is decidedly strained... There are miles of tubing in the basement, there are half-a-dozen men in the area, and half-a-dozen men in the road using inelegant language, and evidently telling each other funny stories... I shall yet be discovered on Essie's doorstep with a portmanteau...*

Mlle. Sans-Gêne, 'Notes from my Diary', *Country Life*, April 1897

The annual renovation was the ideal time to have rooms decorated, and specialist artisans such as stained-glass makers or gilders were often accommodated on the estate. At Sudbury Hall in Derbyshire, in the mid-1850s, the housekeeper was reputedly a very fearsome female, with a booming voice and an authoritarian manner. She took the unilateral decision to 'brighten the place up' while the family was away, and instructed the decorators to paint white the great carved wooden staircase, believed to be one of the finest examples from the seventeenth century in any English country house. The Vernon family were horrified on their return, and insisted that the staircase was stripped and returned to its original appearance.

The return of the family after the big spring clean was not necessarily a happy experience for the servants:

*Wednesday: Hurrah! I am in the best of spirits, having been ordered up to town to superintend the domestic arrangements of the family mansion, and smooth the way for the arrival of my mother and her belongings. My sole notion of putting a house in order is to fill all the vases I can find with the most expensive of flowers. When I have accomplished this, and told the lady in charge of the house to keep the kettle boiling all day and all night, I feel I have done my duty and can go out and meet my various friends with an easy conscience... I left her with a bright smile and a sympathetic nod which meant, 'Get it all finished by the time I come back, and don't bother me.' Then I went out to lunch at Willis's, where the fare is excellent and the red leather seats have an inviting air...*

Mlle. Sans-Gêne, 'Notes from my Diary', *Country Life*, March 1897

111

# Vermin

A perennial problem in the Victorian and Edwardian eras was the proliferation of insects and rodents, especially inside the home.

## Infested beds

Beds and pillows were particularly prone to insect infestation. The mattresses were filled with organic material, horse hair or feathers, and therefore very tempting for bedbugs and fleas. Bedding tended to be thoroughly cleaned twice a year, at the same time as the big spring and autumn house cleanings, but naturally an outbreak of bedbugs in the meantime necessitated a vigorous response. Decent housekeepers checked the bedding every week; any trace of bedbugs required the servants to take the bed apart, to wash the frame with chloride of lime and water and liberally distribute Keating's patent bug-powder over all surfaces and the bedding. Recalcitrant cases might necessitate sealing the room and leaving burning cakes of sulphur inside the room to suffocate the insects. Bedbugs were no respecters of class; even Beatrix Potter, who was such a keen and gifted observer of wildlife, remarked that it was '…possible to have too much Natural History in a bed…', after a sleepless night in an infested Torquay hotel.

## Vermin in kitchens

Vermin could also be a problem in kitchens; to deter black beetles, fleas, crickets and cockroaches, the traditional wooden boards or ceramic tiles were often replaced with a layer of cement, then linoleum, which was hard-wearing, easy to wash and impermeable. Carbolic acid was added to the water used to scrub the floors every day, and neat carbolic was applied to any cracks on a regular basis. *The Servants' Magazine* did not mince its words:

*To destroy Fleas, when they have got into flooring. Handful of salt in a pail of cold water, floor well wetted daily.*

*The Servants Magazine*, August 1857

# Cockroaches

Cockroaches were social climbers; they would travel up the channels accommodating the bell wires and hot-water pipes from the basement into the family's quarters. Before the coming of insecticides, cockroaches were a serious problem in the warmer parts of country houses: the hall boy at Ickworth in Suffolk had the task of sweeping them up and putting them in the boiler, while a kitchen maid at Petworth in Sussex recalled with distaste the underfoot sensation of crunching cockroaches in the dark of the unlit kitchen corridor as she returned home after an illicit evening at a dance.

# Moths

Voracious pests were a fact of everyday life, but frequent airing and 'turning out' of cupboards and drawers helped to keep the problem to a minimum. Mrs Beeton advocated that furs needed to be brushed through vigorously and stored in chests made of camphor wood or sandalwood. Other experts recommended cedar shavings, lavender or twists of pepper.

Housekeepers were similarly hawk-eyed in maintaining their stocks of linens by using dried lavender and camphor, pomanders and cedar-wood blocks, to deter clothes moths. However, there were casualties: Lady Louisa Cavendish took the reluctant decision to have the State Bed in the High Great Chamber at Hardwick Hall destroyed because it was 'entirely devoured by moth'. At Cotehele in Cornwall tapestries were regularly dosed with a home-made concoction boiled up from laurel leaves; it smelt foul and certainly deterred clothes moths.

# Rodents

To keep down rodents, a perennial problem in the kitchen and cellar areas of big country houses, butlers were advised to bait their traps with 'malt flour balls to which is added butter and a drop of aniseed'. Rat-catchers and their terriers might be brought in if the problem was severe; mice were generally kept under control with mousetraps, as 'kitchen' cats tended to be too spoilt and overfed by the staff to be motivated to catch rodents.

Left: An advertisement for Keating's Powder, to rid your clothes and bedding of bugs, fleas, beetles, moths, and other kinds of distressing insects, 1913.

Below: Illustration from *The Universal Directory for Taking Alive and Destroying Rats* (1768) by Robert Smith in the Library at Calke Abbey, Derbyshire.

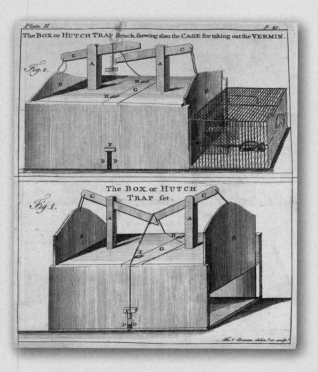

# Fire in country houses

Fire was a constant menace in buildings heated by solid fuel and lit by candles, oil lamps or, later, gas. In 1888 out of every 1,000 fires, more than 200 were due to the upsetting of an oil lamp or candle, or an unguarded candle flame catching some other material alight.

Households of all sizes were constantly reminded of the potential dangers of fire. At Lyme Park, servants were given printed instructions on fire-fighting and prevention:

1. *Be cautious how you use matches and candles. On no account throw a match lighted or unlighted on the floor. See that they are quite extinguished before leaving a room.*
2. *Mind the wind does not blow a curtain over a candle, and that all fire guards are properly on the grate.*
3. *Do not leave any wood, paper, shavings, rags &c. where a fire, or candle can possibly set them alight.*
4. *Report any unusual smoke, or smell of fire to the Butler or Housekeeper.*

Servants were drilled to notice the first signs of a possible conflagration, raise the alarm and where possible tackle the seat of the fire themselves. They were often trained to operate early fire appliances. Some Merryweather fire engines survive at country houses; painted red and complete with brass helmets and hoses, they were kept in the stable yard. However, they relied on an ample source of water nearby, and manpower to operate the hand pumps.

Right: A fire engine inscribed 'His Grace, The Duke of Devonshire, Hardwick Hall' on the side, Hardwick Hall, Derbyshire.

# Conflagrations

There were numerous examples of country seats being reduced to ashes in a matter of hours, despite the desperate efforts of the family, their staff, outdoor servants, estate tenants and helpful neighbours. At Hatfield House in Hertfordshire in 1835 the Dowager Marchioness of Salisbury died in a fire started by her own candle. That an aristocrat could be killed by fire provoked alarm among the landowning classes and created a market for horse-drawn fire engines to be kept on the estate, complete with an experienced crew recruited from the servants.

## Country-house fire brigades

Polesden Lacey in Surrey had its own fire crew, recruited from the male servants, and a fire truck that was stored under the water tower. The staff were paid an extra amount monthly for fire duties, and each time they practised they would get a few shillings more.

Above: Row of red fire buckets in the kitchen hallway at Uppark, West Sussex.

In the nineteenth century Petworth House in Sussex maintained its own fire brigade, engine and pump, staffed by servants. One evening in 1872, the alarm was raised as the offices on the east side of the complex were on fire. The Petworth Fire Brigade, led by the grittily named Captain Death, tackled the fire from the east while the western side was attacked by Lord Leconfield's manual engine and steam pump, operated by the servants. His Lordship supervised operations; all available servants handed buckets of water up the line to the fire engines, and a second line passed them back empty for refilling.

### Advice for servants trapped by fire

The possibility of being trapped on the upper storeys of a house on fire was an ever-present threat. Servants' bedrooms were located in attics, and one very salutary article published in *The Servants' Magazine* in 1856 offered practical advice for such a situation, much of it similar to present-day emergency information, though it did include the following memorable but startling recommendation:

*All persons thus circumstanced are earnestly entreated not to precipitate themselves from the window while there remains the least probability of assistance… in all such cases it is advisable, if possible, to select a window over the doorway, rather than over the area.*

# The impact of technological improvements on servants

So much of the daily workload of domestic servants was repetitive drudgery. Armies of servants transported food, fuel and hot water, took luggage up and down stairs, cleaned acres of floors, walls and carpets, and cooked for scores of people. A footman could cover 29km (18 miles) in a working day without leaving the confines of the house; a housemaid would make repeated journeys up three flights of stairs from the basement, eventually carrying enough water to fill six baths, before making the return journey similarly burdened. The only way to escape hard work was to gain promotion and so direct others to do it.

The problem was not so much the absence of available technology, but rather the attitude of the householder. In large historic houses, the prospect of introducing modern plumbing, central heating or electricity was a daunting and expensive one. Some people clung to the old methods, seeing no need whatsoever to change the habits of several lifetimes while there were still ample supplies of servants to meet all their physical needs.

## World-beating innovations at Cragside

The nineteenth century was a time of innovation and scientific confidence. There were some houses in which technological advances made major improvements to the lives of servants; in fact, at Cragside there were innovations that were the first in the world. William Armstrong harnessed the flowing water from a stream on his property, and invented a hydro-electric power station to create renewable power, the first in the world. Hydro-electricity powered his new house; the lift, of great benefit to the servants, conveyed luggage and coal, meals and furniture between floors, almost effortlessly. There was an electric dishwasher, an unimaginable luxury to most scullery maids, and a roasting spit, which no longer needed to be turned by human agency or rely on the whims of chimney up-draughts. There were even electric dinner gongs. Cragside was the first house in the world to have electric light, introduced in 1878.

When the Prince and Princess of Wales came to stay in 1884, the future Edward VII was amazed; as a dedicated enthusiast for luxurious living, he was also an ambassador for the new technology, and his other wealthy friends were quick to take the hint.

# Electricity

Electricity revolutionised the working lives of servants. Electric lighting eradicated the need to renew and replace oil lamps, candles and accessories, mop up spills, and clean wallpapers, textiles and furniture stained by greasy soot and wax. Electricity for lighting was very expensive to run; consequently until the 1920s it was confined to the homes of the very wealthy. Even at Osterley Park in Middlesex electricity was not introduced until 1925; Lady Jersey preferred to hold receptions in the Gallery lit by 400 candles.

The coming of electricity could be slow to reach the staff; electricity for lighting was installed at Tatton Park, Cheshire, in 1887 to welcome a visit from the Prince and Princess of Wales, but the workers living in the Old Hall on the estate had to do without it until 1958, 71 years later.

### The uses of electricity

In Britain, electricity was limited to urban districts until the late 1920s when the National Grid was established. Interestingly, after its use for lighting, its most common application was for the running of electric irons, one of the more troublesome elements of household maintenance. By the start of the Great War, manufacturers were starting to produce further labour-saving devices, such as washing machines, vacuum cleaners and gas cookers. The coming of the vacuum cleaner was originally rather a novelty: H. Cecil Booth established the British Vacuum Cleaner Company, which provided suction-operated appliances, mounted on horse-drawn vehicles, to customers' houses; the hose was passed through an open window and vacuumed up detritus, which it took away for disposal. Within a few years, it was possible to buy electrically powered appliances for home use.

Below: One of the electric gongs at Cragside (c.1880), which warned guests that meal times were approaching.

117

### Electric servants

By the first decade of the twentieth century the middle classes were suffering from a dearth of domestic servants, and were looking for mechanical assistance. The 'Servant Shortage' was exacerbated by the Great War, and the nascent electricity companies targeted the wealthy with information on the wonders of the new technology. Demonstrators in electricity showrooms showed how householders could use their 'electric servants', proving that an investment in a labour-saving device would reduce a household's reliance on an ever-diminishing supply of willing domestic help. The irony is that the new vacuum cleaners were made in factories staffed by young women who in previous generations would have had no choice but to go into service, and who would otherwise still be sprinkling damp tea leaves on the mistress's carpet and wielding a broom.

Historic houses and their owners remained largely resistant to the enticements of new technology; at Speke Hall near Liverpool central heating was installed in 1895, and hot and cold water supplies, flushing WCs and even a telephone followed shortly after. However the Hall continued to be lit by oil lamps until 1934–5. By contrast in America, electricity was considered a boon from its inception and this may have been because of the differing attitudes to servants; in a more egalitarian society, labour-saving devices were held to be progressive because they reduced the reliance on a designated class to manage the drudgery of domestic life. As Catherine E. Beecher (sister of Harriet Beecher Stowe, author of *Uncle Tom's Cabin*) wrote in 1869, 'In England, the class who go to service are a class, and service is a profession… in America, domestic service is a stepping stone to something higher.'

## Lifts

Electrically powered lifts benefited menservants in particular. Footmen were required to carry trunks and portmanteaux from their delivery at the ground floor level up several flights of stairs to the guest bedrooms. With a large house party arriving and each guest bringing several cases or trunks, this was hard work. There was a luggage lift at Castle Drogo in Devon, powered by hydro-electricity provided by the River Teign in the gorge below the house. At St Michael's Mount, off the Cornish coast, the firm of Merryweather & Sons Ltd installed an oil engine which powered a lift to transport baggage and provisions from the castle's quay, a major improvement. Lift-power caught on: an Otis lift was installed at Waddesdon Manor near Aylesbury for the visit of Queen Victoria in 1891.

# Food from the estate

*All the skill of the most accomplished cook will avail nothing unless she is furnished with prime provisions...*

Anon, *Enquire Within About Everything*, 1890

## Kitchen gardens and the Home Farm

Kitchen gardens provided the household with fresh fruit and vegetables. When the family were staying in London for the Season, produce and flowers from their estates would be dispatched in hampers by train several times a week. Each day the head gardener would advise the cook on what was available, before sending an assistant to fill the order.

Cattle, pigs, poultry, arable crops and timber were produced by the Home Farm. Milk was brought to the dairy twice daily by the dairyman, to be turned into butter, cream or cheese. The shepherd cared for the sheep and the pigman had custody of the swine; these animals were sold at market or slaughtered on site for consumption by the household.

Above: The gardeners at Polesden Lacey, Surrey (c.1928).

## Self-reliance

Remote country houses were largely self-reliant. Llanerchaeron, with its service courtyard complete with dairy, brewery, laundry and kitchen gardens, is a rare survival of an almost totally self-sufficient eighteenth-century estate. Petworth was similarly well-provisioned: the extensive park kept the house supplied with venison, game, eels and fish; the kitchen gardens produced 400 varieties of vegetables, as well as flowers and fruit for the house.

However, local businesses did rely on orders from the country house for non-native substances such as coffee, tobacco, tea and chocolate. Luxuries such as turtle meat or soup, truffles, sea fish, oysters and exotic spices were ordered and delivered to the back door.

# Off the kitchen corridor

## The back door

Every grand household had a 'back door', where supplies from the estate and beyond were delivered daily. This was the start of a production line: raw materials arrived here, were checked for quality and dispatched to storage or for immediate use, passing through specialist hands to their ultimate destination. At Petworth in Sussex, there was a weighing room where the chef could check the weight of ingredients being delivered.

Inside the kitchen complex, an impressive sequence of storage and preparation rooms ran off the main corridor. At Lanhydrock in Cornwall, for example, there are game larders and pastry rooms, wet rooms for the storage of fish (including tanks for live but ultimately doomed marine specimens), and storerooms lined with cupboards for flour, sugar and other 'dry' goods. There is also a spectacular dairy room, where waist-high marble slabs are constantly fed with trickles of cold water; here, desserts and jellies would have been made, allowed to set and then stored for later consumption. Each room had a specific function, and dedicated staff who knew how to handle, store and prepare the food.

## The vegetable store

Just inside the back door at many old houses one often finds a room or an alcove, with waist-high work surfaces and shelves, and pull-out drawers below. These were the vegetable hoppers, where kitchen gardeners delivered the day's provisions for the attention of the scullery maid, who had to prepare them. The gardeners were allowed no further inside the house than the back door, as they were wearing muddy boots.

## The butchery

Hygiene considerations dictated the location of meat larders. Raw meat was stored in small, robust, north-facing rooms with thick, whitewashed walls and wire-gauze mesh over the unglazed windows, to deter flying insects and keep out predators. A utilitarian room, the butchery was fitted with a rack from which joints, game and sides of meat could be hung, a pallet for transporting larger carcasses, and chopping tables for meat preparation, usually done by the odd man or one of the stockmen from the farm. A chopping block was usually provided for smaller-scale butchery.

Right: The game larder at Dunham Massey in Cheshire with various maturing game birds, a hare and a rabbit.

# The game larder

Most large country houses had game larders, where the carcasses of game birds, hares, rabbits and the occasional deer would be hung until deemed 'ripe'.

Experienced cooks prided themselves on finely judging the tipping point at which game was about to 'go over'. This was not a precise science. Former butler 'Fred' Sheppard recalled how his employer, Lord Montagu of Beaulieu, had been given a large haunch of venison as a gift. He had consigned it to the cook to hang in the game larder. However, His Lordship was unavoidably delayed in London for two weeks, and on his return to Hampshire the cook admitted she had disposed of the venison. Taking a spade, Lord Montagu dug the haunch out of the dung heap where it had been interred, hung it on an apple tree and hosed it down, before returning it to the cook and insisting she roast it as instructed. Those who were brave enough to tackle the meat claimed the taste was superb.

# Smoked and preserved meats

Some kitchen complexes had separate larders for salting, smoking or storing bacon. Every autumn pork was salted to make sides of bacon to carry the household through the winter. The pig's carcass was hung to air, then butchered into manageable joints. Each slab of meat would be rubbed all over with bare hands, working to get a combination of salt and a small amount of sugar deeply ingrained into every surface. The meat was buried in a deep tin bath full of salt for several days and then hung from rafters to 'prove' and dry out thoroughly. In some households the pork might also be cured in a smoking room where the fire was fuelled by wood, sawdust and peat, to give it extra flavour.

# The china store

Every country house needed vast quantities of china. The variously sized mixing bowls, basins and pails required in the kitchen tended to be plain white and decorated with a simple 'K'. The servants' quarters had plain and robust earthenware for everyday dining, while the family used decorative sets of matching china. But most households also kept formal sets of china for entertaining, and stored them separately from the everyday stock. The China Room at Penrhyn had walls of cupboards and shelves holding hundreds of pieces of fine china. One single service consists of 114 dinner plates, 22 soup plates, 23 pudding plates, 6 vegetable dishes, 3 soup tureens and 3 sauce tureens.

## Ice houses, refrigeration and ice cream

In the era before electric refrigeration, considerable ingenuity was applied to keeping foodstuffs cold. Country estates often had a designated ice house; in winter the outdoor staff collected slabs of ice or compacted snow, and this was stored in a purpose-built ice house, usually deep underground, as at Ham House, or set into a brick-lined cave in a shady bank, as at Osterley Park. Throughout the year, ice was brought indoors and put into insulated bins in the larders, providing a cold store for temperature-sensitive foods such as jellies and mousses. Vast wine coolers were filled with ice to chill the champagne before social occasions.

Like many large houses, Petworth prided itself on its ability to make intricate and impressive iced desserts. Pewter and tin ice-cream moulds of astonishing complexity survive at the house; hinged two-piece shells produced three-dimensional ice-cream 'fruits', from pineapples to walnuts, asparagus bundles to bunches of grapes.

The chef prepared the mixture, creating a 'custard' of cream and sugar, to which was added various colourings and flavourings. The mixture was put into a cylinder in the centre of a bucket and surrounded with ice and saltpetre. It was left to stand for three hours, and the handle would occasionally be turned, a job usually undertaken by the scullery man. Moulds were filled with the 'iced cream' mixture and closed, then plunged into buckets full of ice and saltpetre until required. Although ice-creams and sorbets were made 'in house', the ice was only used to chill the desserts, as it was too polluted to eat.

## The brew house

One of the perks for both indoor and outdoor servants was access to alcohol, especially in the first half of the nineteenth century. Most large estates maintained their own brew houses, where beer was made for consumption by the whole household. The technique

*That the Men at Breakfast be allowed one pint of Beer or Cyder each, at Dinner and Supper Men & Maids a pint each. Strangers a quart [two pints], no other drinking whatever in the Hall or any other part of the House or out Houses under one Shilling forfeit to each offenders [sic] …if any Servant or Servants while on Master's or Mistress's business or out with them be drunk he or they to forfeit five Shillings…*

From *Rules to be Strictly Observed*, printed rules hanging in the Servant's Quarters at Cotehele, c.1840

of brewing had changed little since the Middle Ages, because the beverage was still an essential part of daily life. Untreated well or spring water could harbour infections and harmful bacteria. Ale and beer were much safer to drink, as the production process requires the mash to be thoroughly boiled before cooling and fermentation.

## 'Strong beer' and 'small beer'

Country-house beers came in two types: 'strong beer' resulted from the first mash; while weaker 'small beer' was produced from the second and third mashes of the reused malt. Small beer was supplied to the servants, the women and children. In the servants' hall, a cask of beer was usually placed on a wheeled trolley on the table during mealtimes, so that the staff could help themselves. In addition, visitors to the servants' quarters could expect to be offered beer: at Chatsworth and Longleat there was always a jug of beer and a plate of cheese on a table in the servants' hall.

Below: The Brew House at Charlecote Park in Warwickshire, typical of a well-ordered English country seat during late eighteenth century. It was used to brew beer for the household until the early twentieth century.

# 4 DAILY DUTIES AND BIG EVENTS

# Breakfast for 'upstairs'

Breakfast had always been a haphazard business in even the grandest houses, but as the men of the Victorian upper classes started to leave the house early and return late, breakfast became a more substantial meal. Hearty appetites were catered for: Sonia Keppel recalled how in the 1890s her father would dispose of two boiled eggs, two fried eggs, an omelette, and kidneys and bacon, followed by copious amounts of buttered toast with jam.

Most country houses had a designated breakfast room, often east-facing to catch the morning light. Family breakfast was usually served between 9 and 10am, immediately after household prayers. The kitchen servants prepared all the hot breakfast foods, which were kept warm below stairs. The food was laid out on the sideboard and the family helped themselves; the footmen stood in attendance in case anything should be required.

## High-protein buffet

In country houses by the mid-nineteenth century, breakfast was a high-protein buffet comprising dishes such as poached, scrambled and coddled eggs, sausages and bacon, kippers, kedgeree and kidneys, fillet steak, fried rabbit and fritters, supplemented with a variety of breads and pastries, toast, butter, jam and marmalade, all to be accompanied by samovars of different types of tea and coffee. A breakfast on this scale was not consumed every morning by every guest; the aim was to provide a rich and attractive cornucopia, a promise of plenty. For the abstemious, there was always porridge. The Great British Breakfast still survives in a modified version in hotels, and is viewed with enthusiasm by many overseas visitors, for whom the native cuisine is otherwise seen as a mixed bag.

Left: A woman plans her day from her bed, while her maid carries a breakfast tray.

## Breakfast in bed

At Petworth House, breakfast was eaten off china, but every other meal was served on silver plate. For weekending lady guests, especially if their menfolk had disappeared early to go shooting, breakfast was a leisurely affair to be enjoyed in bed. The gardeners there provided a large basket of nosegays, one of which was added to each lady's breakfast tray for decoration.

In the 1880s at Uppark, the mistress, Lady Fetherstonhaugh (the former dairymaid) and her sister particularly relished having their breakfasts brought up to them in bed at 9am, so they could enjoy 'butter and fancy breads, creams, Devonshire cream etc., on lovely silver and china plates, butter dishes, cheese stands, folded serviettes…'

125

# Ladies' lunches and domestics' dinners

Mrs Beeton was non-committal about luncheon, seeing it as a necessary if somewhat unappealing opportunity to use up leftovers from the previous day.

## The 'upstairs' lunch

By the late nineteenth century, the 'upstairs' lunch was seen by the élite leisured classes as an acceptable way of providing hospitality and of meeting one's social obligations without incurring vast expense; a perfect way to entertain single ladies and elderly ladies, whom one was not obliged to 'pair' with suitable gentlemen, and to try out new acquaintances, to check their social acceptability. In time, in the grandest homes even lunch took on the dimensions of a substantial Christmas dinner, easily stretching to eight courses.

# Afternoon tea

Afternoon or '5 o'clock' tea came about because the nineteenth-century dinner moved from late afternoon to mid-evening. It was a long time between luncheon at 1pm and dinner at 7.30pm or 8pm. To fill the gap, ladies of leisure were inclined to order a tray of tea and a few snacks to be consumed discreetly in their boudoir or bedroom in the later afternoon.

By 1850, the fashionable were consuming afternoon tea with guests in the drawing room, conservatory or garden, served by the footman or butler. On regular afternoons of the week, ladies would let it be known they were 'at home' to selected callers.

The kitchen staff provided small dainty sandwiches, biscuits, gingerbread, chocolate cakes, *petits fours* and scones, and the practice effectively put an end to the cook's opportunity for an afternoon nap or a gossip with her own visitors. In some households the cook was even required to change her outfit, don a fresh apron and help serve the guests with water ices or cakes from a buffet in the drawing room. The mistress of the house had custody of the silver teapot, with a supporting role being played by the butler or footman, who would proffer teacups, plates and snacks. Beverley Nichols recalled the afternoon teas at Polesden Lacey:

*Left: The Tea Room at Polesden Lacey in Surrey, displaying some of Mrs Greville's smaller items of French furniture from her London house.*

*Tea is at 5 o'clock… and not at 5 minutes past… which means the Spanish Ambassador, who has gone for a walk down the yew avenue, hastily retraces his steps, and the Chancellor of the Exchequer… hurries down the great staircase, and that the various gentlemen rise from their chaise-longues… and join the procession to the tea-room. The tea-pots, cream-jugs, the milk-pots and the sugar basins are of Queen Anne silver; the tea service is Meissen; and the doilies, heavily monogrammed, are of Chantilly lace… Maggie's teas were terrific, with great Georgian teapots and Indian or China, and muffins and cream cakes and silver kettles sending up their steam, and Queen Mary saying 'Indian, if you please, and no sugar'…*

Beverley Nichols, *The Sweet and Twenties*, 1958

Afternoon tea became a milestone in the daily round of the grand house; in some places it was more of a millstone. At Ickworth, near Bury St Edmunds, all the family and their guests were expected to be present for tea, at the appointed hour, unless they had formally asked in advance to be excused.

# Dressing for dinner

The dinner gong was the signal to the family and their house guests that it was time to repair to their rooms for a hot bath, and to change into more formal garb for the evening. The period allowed at each house between dressing gong and dinner gong varied, but it was usually at least 45 minutes. It was also the signal to the nursery that any junior inhabitants should now be on their way to bed.

At Ickworth in Suffolk, as at most grand houses, the family dressed for dinner every evening. The meal was usually at 8 o'clock, but it was put back to 8.30pm in the summer because the Marchioness liked to be outside for as long as possible. This preference was resented by the servants, who had to stay up later in order to have everything cleared, washed up, and put away in preparation for the morning.

Following the gong, in more technologically advanced households with plumbing, a servant would run a bath for 'their' lady or gentleman; valets might be required to act as barbers, and all menservants of a certain rank would lay out a gentleman's evening clothes and accessories such as cufflinks while he was bathing, as a matter of course. Butlers with foresight also sent up a generous aperitif or two: a whisky with water was generally acceptable, but individual preferences were accommodated and often noted in the butler's notebooks for future reference. Menservants were wise to ascertain a gentleman's preferred tipple and any other idiosyncrasies, to be assured of a decent tip.

## Dressing duties: men

The valet's role was to help 'his' gentleman to dress, and to check his final appearance from all angles, wielding a clothes brush to raise the nap of his evening jacket so that it appeared suitably matt in texture. Some men found their collar studs fiddly and their starched collars tricky to attach; white ties could be difficult to tie symmetrically, and the white piqué waistcoats worn under dinner 'coats' needed adjusting with tapes at the back of the waist to achieve a smooth, unwrinkled frontage. Ready at last, the diner would descend to the drawing room. The valet would pick up the day's discarded clothes and footwear, and sort them into dirty linen bound for the laundry or items to be ironed, brushed, steamed and worn again.

# Dressing duties: ladies

Ladies had a trickier time completing their toilette: following the bath, they needed help to get dressed again. A simple shift went next to the skin, then the corset, crucial to the underpinnings of any outfit; as this laced in the centre of the back, an experienced second pair of hands was needed. The pantaloons in place, the lady might then put on hoops, a crinoline or a bustle, each of which gave a specific sculptural shape to her outer garments.

## Changing fashions

By the 1870s, the circular crinoline had been supplanted by a variety of bustles and 'crinolettes', skeletal contraptions designed to hold out the wearers' skirts at the back. Manufacturers gave each model an aspirational name such as the 'Lady Eleanor', or the memorable 'Parisian Collapsing Princess'.

Topped by petticoats, and with stockings held up by garters or suspenders attached to the lower edge of the corset, the lady and her maid would now tackle the dress. Skirts to go on top of hoops or crinolines were put on over the head. Dresses of a narrower cut were 'concertinaed' on to a sheet laid on the floor, and the lady would step carefully into the centre of the garment, standing still while the maid gently pulled it up to shoulder level. The maid might add cotton pads under the armpits to emphasise the desirable 'wasp waist', and also to act as a barrier to underarm perspiration.

Once the dress was in place, and done up, the hair could be dressed. Evening shoes were generally designed to match the dress, and made of kid or satin. Jewellery was a necessity and was considered carefully; valuable pieces were usually stored in the household safe and needed to be extracted in preparation for the evening. Long white gloves completed the ensemble; Madam was ready for dinner.

*From the direction of the hall there came a new sound, faint at first but swelling and swelling to a frenzied blare, seeming to throb through the air with a note of passionate appeal like a woman wailing for her demon lover. It was that tocsin of the soul, that muezzin of the country-house, the dressing-for-dinner gong.*

P.G. Wodehouse, *Summer Lightning*, 1929

Above: Portrait of *Alda Weston, Lady Hoare* (1910) by St George Hare, at Stourhead, Wiltshire. She is wearing appropriate dinner attire.

# 'Dinner is served'

Dinner as the main meal of the day was literally a 'moveable feast', depending on the needs and habits of the household. In the eighteenth century, the main meal of the day might be served any time between noon and about 2pm, taking advantage of the best of the daylight available. In the evening, the household would have a less elaborate supper by candlelight.

By the 1830s and 40s, 'dinner' was hovering irresolutely around 4pm, which satisfied no one, as some kind of supper was needed in the evening. The coming of paraffin lamps and gaslight expanded the evening into time to be spent socialising. Dinner in polite circles finally settled at about 8pm. For servants, their main meal would be taken around midday or early afternoon, supplemented by a substantial supper in the evening.

## Dinner duties

The family would congregate in the drawing room to receive their guests; if it was a large party, each gentleman would be 'matched' with an introduction to the lady he was to escort into dinner. At exactly 8pm, the butler would announce that 'Dinner is served, ma'am'. The host would lead the procession into the dining room, with the most important lady on his arm; matched pairs would follow suit, and the hostess would bring up the rear with the principal male guest.

## Formal dinners

A formal dinner was a lengthy and often luxurious affair in most households. All the participants would be on their best behaviour, the table looking magnificent and the staff immaculately turned out. Freshly bathed, the gentlemen would be in white tie and tails; the ladies in full-length gowns with jewellery glittering discreetly; the candles flickering on the silver and crystal enticingly; the menu would be handwritten in French, and any small children were safely bedded down in the nurseries, several storeys away.

Service at table was swift, virtually silent and as polished as the silver. For formal dinners, a footman stood behind the chair of each lady diner, so that chairs might be held out for them and slid gently under them as they sat down. The butler generally stood throughout

the meal 'on guard' behind his hostess's chair, directing the servants with almost imperceptible movements, and administering the distribution of the wine. The footmen would serve wine from the right and food from the left; they would hold each dish so that the guest could help themselves from it easily.

### *À la française*

For the first half of the nineteenth century, formal dinners tended to be served by a long-standing system known as *à la française*, in which, in succession, one of three impressive courses, each consisting of many dishes, would be laid simultaneously on the table, and the guests would be exhorted to help themselves and their neighbours from a vast array of accompanying dishes placed with them. This system had its drawbacks, as the guests on one side of the table were reliant on those on the other to hand to them what they wanted, which they often omitted to do if the conversation was animated or the party was large, so there was a great deal of waste. The servants would then remove all the dishes from the first course and replace them simultaneously with all the food for the next course.

Above: Dining table laid with dinner service and candles in the ground-floor Dining Room at Attingham Park, Shropshire.

131

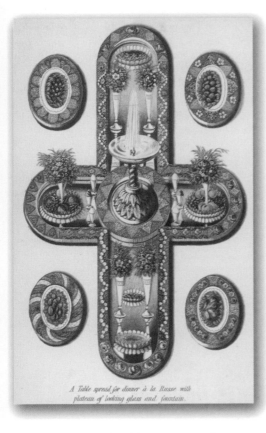

A Table spread for dinner à la Russe with
plateau of looking glass and fountain.

Above: A table
spread for dinner *à
la russe* with plateau
of looking glass and
fountain (c.1840).

### À la russe

By the late nineteenth century, dinner was more often
served *à la russe*, with a single course at a time dispensed
by the servants at side tables and then handed around
the guests, each of whom would help themselves, or
be helped by footmen, to accompanying dishes. This
format avoided the inevitably bacchanalian scene of
half-consumed dishes littering the entire table at the
end of each course. It allowed free rein to the hostess
to show off her elaborate table decorations, flowers and
silver, and was evidence of the number of servants in her
household, and their polished expertise. Service *à la russe*
made the diners dependent on the servants for assistance
with every aspect of the meal; to be waited on 'hand, foot
and finger' set new benchmarks in luxury and underlined
the distinction between the served and the servants.

### The food

Every guest had a handwritten menu at their place
setting. For those pacing themselves to survive eight
or nine courses, in their tight-laced evening corsets or
restrictive cummerbunds, this was useful information.
It was quite acceptable for diners to eat only very small
amounts of each course, or to skip a course completely.
In some circles, it was considered *gauche* to comment on the food,
even it if was spectacular; people of sophisticated tastes were
accustomed to fine dining, and not especially interested in food.
As lyricist W.S. Gilbert said, 'It isn't so much what's on the table
that matters, as what's on the chairs.' This lack of appreciation
baffled many a French chef working in the British kitchens, and
drove them to ever-more spectacular efforts to impress.

### Service customs

It had been customary for diners to retain their cutlery, using knife
and fork rests between courses. This practice had died out in Britain
by the beginning of the twentieth century, but continued elsewhere;
a Canadian waitress is reputed to have said to visiting British royalty,
'Keep your fork, Duke, there's pie'.

When service was provided *à la française*, the tablecloth was swiftly
and expertly removed by the footmen after each main course, to
reveal another, identical white cloth underneath; therefore each
of the two main courses and the dessert was known as a *relevé*, or
'remove', as everything on the table was taken away at the same time.

At dessert, the table might be cleared completely, to reveal the polished wood of the table beneath. To prevent this surface being scratched by dessert bowls, flannel squares were placed under the plates. These, having been invented by a London draper with the name of D'Oyley, were known by the servants as 'doilies'.

## The hostess's role

The hostess paced her consumption of each course to match that of the slowest diner, because as soon as she finished eating, the guests were obliged out of politeness to stop, and the plates would be cleared. Queen Victoria, who was always served first at any meal and would immediately begin to eat, was unaware that court protocol dictated that once she had cleared her plate, all her guests would stop too, until one brave and hungry soul had a discreet tussle with the footman who was attempting to remove his unfinished food. The Queen noticed, enquired the reason, and subsequently the practice was abandoned.

After dinner, the hostess would 'catch the eye' of the most important female guest so that they would simultaneously stand, inviting the other ladies to retire to the drawing room. The gentlemen at the table would move seats so as to sit nearer the host, consume port or brandy and cigars and talk business. The ladies would be served tea or coffee, maybe even cigarettes, by the footmen, while the butler would serve the gentlemen. The men would sooner or later rejoin the ladies in the drawing room; if they showed no such inclination, after a while the hostess would order coffee to be sent in to them, a heavy hint. Finally reunited with the distaff side, the men might settle for tea, but a decent hostess ensured that punch was also available, as well as a little supper, in case anyone was still peckish.

## Staff roles

With her secretary or housekeeper, the hostess selected the guests' placement according to rank and social compatability. The cook would submit a suggested menu for approval, and the butler was responsible for the table and the wine. The housekeeper or head housemaid ensured that the house was immaculate. The white-gloved butler laid out the table with military precision, measuring the exact distance between cutlery and stemware. Floral arrangements would be brought in, then the table was augmented with place cards and menus. Hostesses prided themselves on orchestrating perfection; in fact it was usually the attention to detail and practical experience of a team of professional servants that ensured success.

# Balls and parties

Grand houses were ideal places in which to hold large parties, and there were many excuses for a ball. In London, a mansion might be used for a daughter's 'coming out' ball, a formal event that signified she was now launched into society and eligible for marriage. On country estates, the household was more likely to celebrate the heir achieving his majority, or to mark engagements or weddings. The scale of these events could be enormous.

## Preparations

The staff were required to work harder and longer than usual if the party was to be successful, and planning would start months in advance. Massive preparations were typically required for a grand ball; local staff would be engaged for the night to assist with washing up, and beds needed to be provided for visiting musicians. Most houses had a room suitable for use as a ballroom, and a substantial supper was always provided in an adjacent room, supplemented by food and drink until the early hours. Champagne was usually served, and the butler or house steward would attempt to manage supplies of drink, chivvying both the regular staff and the temporary waiters. A specialist chef might be brought in with his assistants to organise the food, although this arrangement could cause ill feeling if the resident cook objected.

On special occasions, large households hired agency staff. The grander London houses often kept spare sets of livery to be worn by temporary footmen, and requested 'temps' with the right physique to fit existing outfits; agencies supplied footmen who were at least 5ft 10in (1.7m) tall, preferably 6ft (1.8m). As many as 20 or 30 extra footmen might be required; they were interviewed on site by the butler, kitted out with a set of livery that more or less fitted, and briefed about the layout of the house, the cloakrooms and kitchens, service corridors and backstairs, and the most important people working or living there. Whether serving food or drink, receiving guests or dealing with carriages, they worked until the early hours before returning their livery and being paid off. The most junior kitchen staff found it particularly hard, as on occasions they stayed up so late to clear away the last traces of the festivities that they had no opportunity to go to bed before the next long day's work began.

# Shooting parties

Hunting, fishing and shooting had long been the domain of rural landowners. The development of the railways made it much easier to travel by rail to visit a great house for a few days' shooting. By the 1880s and 1890s, shooting had become a leisure activity much pursued by men of the upper classes.

The Prince of Wales bought Sandringham in Norfolk in 1862 because of its potential to become one of the best hunting lodges in Britain. The number of game killed there crept up from 7,000 to 30,000 a year. His son, the future George V, was even more keen, managing to kill over 1,000 birds in a single day by his own efforts. And for variety, there were grouse and deer to be shot in Scotland.

## The shooting season

The Glorious Twelfth – 12 August – marked the start of the shooting season. Partridges, grouse and pheasants featured on country-house menus throughout the autumn. So massive was

Below: *A Shooting Party at Ranton Abbey* (1840) by Sir Francis Grant, PRA, in the Verandah Passage at Shugborough Hall. The 1st Earl of Lichfield is mounted on the white pony.

the scale on which birds were reared, that shooting them as they flew over the lines of marksmen was not difficult. J.G. Ruffer, author of *The Big Shots: Edwardian Shooting Parties* (1977), remarked that it was like '…the opportunities of a Vimy Ridge machine-gunner with an infinitely better lunch'.

# Running shooting parties

Those of the future king's aristocratic friends who could afford it ran shooting parties in season so that the monarch and his selected circle could stay. Consequently, the indoor servants in the great houses were accustomed to accommodating large numbers of visitors. A sporting gentleman might bring his favourite loader, perhaps his chauffeur, or his valet. Meanwhile his wife could not possibly travel without her lady's maid, so every pair of guests inevitably brought at least two servants. Generally the servants enjoyed shooting parties; it was a break from the household routine, and brought interesting new people into the servants' hall, where news and gossip could be traded, a welcome addition to a remote country house.

### The arrangements

Any shoot generated a great deal of extra work for the servants. At the Boxing Day pheasant shoot at Lyme Park for example, more than 100 people would sit down to lunch. The butler oversaw the arrangements of the party as far as the house was concerned, by ensuring the smooth arrival and departure of guests and by organising where they would sleep. For the footmen, there was more silver to clean than usual, and special china to be washed. In addition, they carried enormous amounts of the guests' luggage up and down stairs, and valeted any man who had not brought his own attendant. The housemaids had more fires to light, and more rooms to clean. On occasions, upper housemaids were pressed into assisting visiting ladies travelling without a lady's maid of their own.

# Women at shooting parties

Shooting was predominantly a male sport, though some women were willing to take part and were considered slightly racy for doing so. While the men set out in Norfolk jackets, plus fours and gaiters, flat caps and stout brogues, most female guests would have a leisurely morning, recovering from the inevitable late night before and being pampered by their maids. There were usually a few non-sporting men who had been invited to keep the social mix interesting. The ladies generally joined the shooting party for a lunch *al fresco*, dressed in suitably rustic-looking tweeds, departing in a succession of horse-drawn vehicles around midday.

## Shooting-party lunches

By the Edwardian era, shooting-party lunches were grand affairs. The Powis Castle estate in Powys once had one of the finest game shoots in the country, attracting members of the Royal Family. As a former kitchen maid working there in 1900 recalled:

*When the shooting parties started the Cook would find out how many guns were taking part and how many ladies were lunching with them as a hot lunch was sent out to them every day… this was packed in big boxes. A special dinner service and table silver was kept for the purpose. Two footmen would be sent out to serve it at one of the lodges nearest the shoot which could be some distance away and was taken by horse-drawn vehicle. This would come back by about 4.30 to 5.00pm, be taken to the pantry, washed and packed ready for the next day.*

At Penrhyn Castle, the huge house parties staying for pheasant shooting in November kept the kitchen staff exceptionally busy. Each shoot typically lasted three days, normally Tuesday, Wednesday and Thursday. Luncheon was served in the open air if the weather was fine, on specially erected tables set with chairs, linen, silver and china. Usually the lunch was held close to a hunting lodge so that use could be made of the 'facilities' if required. If the weather was inclement, the lunch might be set up inside the lodge or in the largest room of the head gamekeepers' cottage.

The food was loaded outside the kitchen into a pony-drawn cart, and dispatched to the site where it was to be consumed. First courses were kept hot in straw-lined boxes; casseroles, stews and curries were favoured, along with game pies and hams, and jacket potatoes. Desserts were weighty puddings such as spotted dick or apple dumplings. Wine, beer and cider were provided as beverages, with sloe gin to accompany the plum cake and cheese. The beaters were supplied with great hunks of bread and cheese while the loaders had joints of meat and jacket potatoes.

Left: *The Crack Shot or The Rifle Range* (1869) by James Tissot, from Wimpole Hall, Cambridgeshire.

Above: Partridge beaters at Holkham Hall in Norfolk (c.1898).

### Beating

Shooting parties were a welcome break from routine for all male servants. At Lyme Park, at least 50 beaters were recruited for the December pheasant shoots. They would spend a day beating, earn a few extra shillings and see some sport. They might also pick up tips from the guests, or receive a brace of pheasants or grouse to take home to their families.

### A full house

Any substantial house with a decent shoot would find itself packed to capacity in season – when the Duke of Devonshire's guests arrived at Hardwick Hall for their annual shooting party in the autumn, they brought along a veritable army of servants. Every available room was occupied, and the visiting footmen were housed in the turrets, which were only accessible across the narrow duckboards placed on the pitched roofs, still in place today, still alarming, and, of course, unlit after dark. 'There was no gas or electricity, and the darkness of the rooms, lit only by a small lamp, was terrifying,' recalled Lady Maud Baillie.

### Hanging and plucking

Pheasants were left unplucked and hung by their necks in the game larder until they were very high, as this was believed to impart an intense flavour; any maggots were disregarded, as they would be killed during the cooking process. When plucking, first the entrails were removed, then the carcass was plunged into very hot water to help remove the feathers, which had to be pulled out in the direction in which they lay, to avoid disfiguring the skin of the bird. The lowest kitchen maid might be given this task, with assistance from the scullery maid or even the hall boy or kitchen boy.

# Travel and servants

*Our plan is to go thro' France, by Cannes… & then proceed to Rome, partly by land, partly by sea, as the fancy takes us. I have done nothing about a Courier yet, not knowing exactly what I was going to do – & now I think I shall very likely be able to do without, as I believe my butler, a capital servant, has been abroad and speaks Italian. I was only told this just now – & have not yet had time to mention the subject to him – but if he does it wd. be better, & less expensive, to take him with us, & engage a laquais de place for the time we are there. Do you not think so? My maid is an experienced traveller, and Ernestine is a Swiss girl, very quick and handy…*

Letter from Caroline Augustus Edgcombe at Cotehele in Cornwall to her brother Henry, 1863

## Travel overseas

Overseas travel was a perk of the job for certain senior servants, but staff accompanying their employers knew that their role was to smooth the family's path and cushion them from any inconvenience. Opportunities abounded as cross-Atlantic shipping made the New World more accessible. Meanwhile, a lengthy period of European peace at the end of Victoria's reign coupled with the worldly geniality of the Prince of Wales (the future Edward VII) made the English *'milords'* welcome all over the Continent. Aristocrats often 'took a cure' at a European spa, a fortnight of therapies, diets, massages and water treatments by day, and glittering social occasions by night. Fashionable British high society would decamp to Europe for holidays, accompanied by their chauffeur and lady's maid, the valet and butler, and even the children, governess, nanny and nursemaid. Inevitably, a visit to Paris was essential for ordering additions to Her Ladyship's wardrobe. Smarter British women bought their clothes in Paris, at houses such as Worth, but would not wear them for a year; the intervening twelve months allowed prevailing fashions to catch up, so that the wearer would not look or feel outlandishly *avant-garde* on her return to Britain.

Above: Bags, riding boots, brogues and top hat which belonged to the 6th Earl of Belmore at Castle Coole, Enniskillen.

# Travel from one residence to another

*As a family we always seemed to be packing and unpacking as we moved from one house to the next. We thought it all quite normal, but it must have been an extraordinary feat of organisation for the servants as each of us children had our ponies who would always travel with us. There were our nannies, nursemaids and grooms, and for the older children there were the French and German governesses. For us it was all great fun, and it wasn't as unsettling as it might have been as we always had our parents and the same servants with us.*

Lady Blanche Cobbald, quoted by John Pearson in *Stags and Serpents*, 1983

Travel within Britain was a treat for lesser servants; having been recruited from local communities, sooner or later they might have a chance to go further afield with 'their' family. The kitchen maid at Penrhyn Castle in 1900, Annie Evans, recalled:

*We used to go to London quite often, to Lord Penrhyn's London house… We travelled second class – there were three classes then. This was particularly when Lord Penrhyn was attending the House of Lords.*

Petworth in the nineteenth century was a very imposing estate, and the family owned land in Yorkshire and the Lake District, as well as property in London, so frequently moved between their various houses, taking with them the valet, lady's maid, footmen, chef and kitchen staff. The housekeeper, housemaids and the house steward would usually stay in Sussex, as would the outdoor staff, to run the estate and care for the house.

People of fashion observed the Season, the annual round of race meetings and hunting and shooting, court balls and London socialising. For certain months of the year the gentry would flock to one place or another to pursue their mutual interests. Needless to say, they would have to take a large entourage of servants.

The Robartes family divided their time between three main residences: they owned Wimpole Hall in Cambridgeshire for a time and a house in London's Belgrave Square, as well as their vast 'country cottage', Lanhydrock in Cornwall. They travelled with their key servants, leaving a skeleton staff at each place to maintain the property, and organise cleaning and redecoration.

# Royal visits

It was a considerable accolade for a grand house to have royal visitors, and servants would be anxious to make sure that everything ran faultlessly so as to impress the guests and their attendants.

## The royal family at Penrhyn

Penrhyn was a favourite haunt of the British royal family. The 2nd Lord Penrhyn hosted the future King Edward VII and Queen Alexandra and their daughters for a four-day visit in July 1894.

The task was immense. The kitchens and larders were stuffed to capacity with hundreds of dishes ready for the first evening. Twenty-six bedrooms were prepared to accommodate the principal guests, including the Duke of Westminster, the Earls of Powis and Denbigh, and six lords. There were 35 house guests, and each of those had brought their own servants, valets or lady's maids, so even the ample accommodation of Penrhyn was packed to capacity.

Over the four days encompassing the royal visit, the staff served more than 1,150 individual meals. Half of these were provided for the servants, both resident and visiting, but in addition the kitchen staff produced 89 dishes of the highest cuisine for the 35 house guests. It was a triumph of organisation, and a great coup for Lord Penrhyn and his family.

### Royal appreciation

Endless care would be taken by a household entertaining royalty to ensure that they would be impressed by the virtuosity of the kitchen staff. A word of appreciation was remembered and treasured. At Powis Castle, the kitchen maid

Below: The Royal visit of King Edward VII and Queen Alexandra at Treasurer's House, York, in 1894.

141

'C.M.B.', who had started work there in 1900 retained fond memories of a particular royal visit:

*The late King George and Queen Mary stayed for a few days; they were then Duke and Duchess of York, and the Duke being a naval man the sweet the first evening was in his honour and it was in the form of a yacht. It was made from Genoese pastry. The outside was covered with Neapolitan violets and filled inside with pistachio nut ice. The masts were of spun sugar and it was daintily decorated. The next morning there was a note on her Ladyship's breakfast tray which read 'the Duchess would like to say that she thought the sweet last evening "A confection of loveliness".'*

## Royals dropping in

Both before and after his accession, King Edward VII was keen on dropping in on the better sort of country house, often with little notice and trailing a large retinue. On a Sunday morning in July 1908 Waldorf Astor received a telephone call announcing that the King planned to visit Cliveden in Buckinghamshire that afternoon. As Nancy Astor remarked, '…I do think it slightly strong bringing 16 people, it made us 40 for tea…'

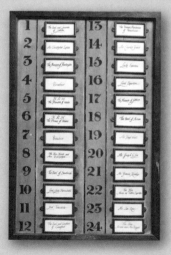

Below: The room number board in the servants' area at Tatton Park, Cheshire. The room plan shows who was staying in each room during the visit of the Prince and Princess of Wales in 1887.

Edward VII was kind and considerate to his servants, though a stickler for protocol and correct behaviour. He always travelled with two valets, and was fond of staying in opulent and entertaining households. Aspirational hostesses took the hint and upgraded their facilities accordingly. One society lady was utterly crushed when fishing for compliments about the vastly expensive bathroom suite newly installed for the Prince's visit. Was it not the ultimate in luxury and convenience? Was there any way at all in which it could bettered? 'Yes', said the future monarch, thoughtfully, 'As a matter of fact, there is no hook on the back of the bathroom door…'

Entertaining the Prince of Wales was an expensive business. In December 1882, the agent at Gunton Park in Norfolk received a letter in which the Prince invited himself to the property for the Christmas shoot. This was a blow to Lord Suffield, whose continuing friendship with the Prince was beginning to cost him dearly. A party of this size would require the household to engage many more staff on a temporary basis and to lavish money on feeding and entertaining his extensive entourage. It appears that either Lord Suffield or his agent concocted a cunning plan to postpone the royal visit by claiming that smoke from a minor fire had damaged the house and that, pending redecorations, regrettably they could not accommodate the royal party. However, to add authenticity to the tale, a maid was instructed to burn some paper in the corner of one of the bedrooms; but the fire got out of control. Although the estate fire engine was quickly deployed, it transpired that it had never been used before and its hoses were not long enough to reach the nearby lake. The resulting damage was disastrous and half the house was burned to the ground. At least the Prince of Wales, with his entourage, was persuaded to take his Christmas holidays elsewhere.

## Professional pride

To senior servants, it was a source of great pride to serve a member of the royal family. Vita Sackville-West, who grew up at Knole, understood their sense of privilege from contact with the monarch, no matter how fleeting. This was an age of great patriotism and national pride, and the merest brush with royalty represented the pinnacle of the professional servant's life. She wrote a knowing portrait of a fictional duchess's secretary, Miss Wace, who was thrilled to work in a house to which the King was such a frequent visitor. Miss Wace feigned reluctance at listing all the preparations and hard work necessitated by a royal visit:

Above: *Royal Visit 1884* by Henry Hetherington Emmerson. The Prince of Wales, later Edward VII, sits on the terrace at Cragside in Northumberland.

*'You would think the servants by now were accustomed to this sort of thing – six visits we had, I think, last year – but would you believe it, something is always forgotten.' It was fair to assume, however, that there were compensations for her extra trouble, for upon the left side of her thin and Republican bosom hung a mauve enamel watch from a true lover's knot of mauve enamel ribbon. 'I have to wear it face outwards', she would explain, 'because of the initials on the back. So silly. Such a pity. It would have been so much nicer plain,' and then she would turn the watch over and display the interlaced E.R.VII, and the crown on the back. 'Of course, I don't like it,' she would say, 'but it's a good little time-keeper, and so I wear it.' In point of fact, everybody knew that it was not a good little time-keeper at all, but gained about an hour a day.*

Vita Sackville-West, *The Edwardians*, 1930

# Christmas in the Big House

In the early Victorian era, Christmas was not widely celebrated as a feast day, but it gradually became an important annual event. By the turn of the century, it was an opportunity for fun and leisure, presents and over-eating, with family and friends. Edwardian Christmases at Lyme Park in Cheshire were a magical time of year:

*...there would be the Christmas tree with all its presents; games in the drawing-room, music and dancing in the hall, private theatricals in the Long Gallery; hide-and-seek all over the house, with people chasing each other in delicious terror the whole length of long corridors; wonderful meals in the dining room, dinners as well as luncheons even for little girls, and all the time everybody, particularly the grown-ups, happy, good-humoured, joking and jolly, ready at any moment to romp and play the fool.*

Phyllis Elinor Sandeman, *Treasures on Earth*, 1952

## Christmas parties

The children's Christmas party at Lyme was remembered with fondness by Annie Crossland. After tea in the servants' hall, lit specially for the occasion with Chinese lanterns, the children of servants and estate workers would be led up to the Long Gallery. Lady Newton, magnificently dressed and wearing a tiara, would distribute presents to each child, with the help of the butler, Mr Truelove. There was an enormous, heavily decorated Christmas tree, adorned by the butler with lit candles. Standing by were two footmen holding damp mops on canes, to extinguish any small fires. Annie's mother taught her to curtsey to Lady Newton, and made her practise for weeks before the annual event. Servants' children in many large houses were often provided with an orange or a small toy, distributed by the mistress, the whole experience fuelled by a big tea eaten 'below stairs'.

At Christmas parties for servants, everyone received a present; this might be a dress length for each of the women, or a sum of money to each of the men. At Chatsworth each male servant was given a piece of beef and a loaf of bread, distributed from a large shed in the wood yard. The maids were offered a choice of stockings, gloves or an umbrella; one brave housemaid asked for a woollen vest.

Right: Christmas tree and traditional presents and toys at Polesden Lacey, Surrey.

# 5 SERVANTS' LIVES

## Recruiting servants

Acquiring and keeping reliable indoor servants was a constant headache in most households; in grand establishments the master or mistress ratified the appointment of the senior staff, while juniors were recruited and interviewed by the butler, housekeeper or cook, according to their occupation.

Bringing a virtual stranger into one's home was a risk, therefore the provision of a satisfactory 'character' was essential if a servant wanted to secure a new post. This handwritten reference commented on the servant's capability, morality, trustworthiness, cleanliness, habits and health. Without a character, a servant was unlikely to get another job. Mistresses often colluded with their least-reliable servants to supply a passable reference so that the inadequate servant could move on. Forgeries were common, so wary mistresses favoured applicants who had stayed in their last place for at least two years, and would write to the previous employer for confirmation.

### Recruitment agencies

In rural areas, the custom had been to find house-servants, as well as agricultural ones, at hiring fairs. By the nineteenth century, advertisements were more widely used; *The Times* or *The Morning*

*Post* ran 'posts wanted' notices, placed by servants. Some favoured asking one's friends and acquaintances, as well as existing members of staff and local tradespeople, to find a reliable and experienced servant. Enterprising individuals set up recruitment agencies for servants; some were notorious for the variable quality of their clients and their rapacity, as the rapid turnover of lower and middle-ranking staff provided commissions from both employer and employee. But reliable agencies did thrive: the Harpur Crewe family of Calke Abbey dealt with Mrs Moseley's agency for servants in nearby Derby for more than 20 years. Sometimes an agency placed a carefully worded newspaper advert to attract a high-calibre candidate. The location of the country-house estate was not revealed, though usually the name of the county in which the house was situated would be included, in case that might prove to be an obstacle. At Petworth in Sussex, servants were often sourced through an agency and many came from some distance away: Mrs Rawlinson, the housekeeper in the 1880s was originally from East Colne in Essex, while her stillroom maid, Mary Bell, was from Bedfordshire. At Ickworth in Suffolk, higher-ranking servants also tended to come from further afield. The censuses of 1871–1901 show that estate workers were locally born but most indoor servants came from outside Suffolk. Similarly, at Lyme Park in Cheshire, Dora Addison recalled that the family provided employment for local people, but also recruited senior staff from further afield:

*There were twenty house servants in the Hall before the Great War. There were the rich and the poor then. Some were poorer people; they got their living and a tiny wage, so it was a good thing. The servants always came from away. The under-people were local. The chief people were from away, they worked themselves up in those days.*

Kedrun Laurie, *Cricketer Preferred: Estate Workers at Lyme Park, 1898–1946*, 1980

Left: A licence for one male servant issued by the Inland Revenue at Castle Cary, Somerset (1891). A government tax was imposed on the employers of menservants from the 1770s to the 1930s and was bitterly resented.

# Poaching staff

Tempting senior staff away from the household of an acquaintance in order to employ them oneself was frowned on in polite circles, but as the shortage of servants began to bite in the early years of the twentieth century, scruples were occasionally overlooked. A discreet enquiry from the lady of the household to her lady's maid or housekeeper often elicited useful information about the servants in neighbouring properties and rival establishments, and overtures could be made.

Above: *The Hon. Mrs Ronald Greville* by Emile Carolus-Duran painted at the time of her marriage in 1891.

Journalist and social commentator Beverly Nichols was a regular house guest of well-connected people all over Britain, and he waspishly observed the undercurrents:

*Those were days when women really did ensnare each other's chefs and kidnap each other's head-gardeners, and offer the most shameless bribes to each other's 'treasures'. (The word 'treasure' is charmingly period. In the upper classes it implied the perfect Jeeves or the ideal nanny. In the middle classes it usually referred to a housemaid or a cook.)*

Beverly Nichols, *Sweet and Twenties*, 1958

Nichols was tickled by the outrage expressed by Mrs Ronnie Greville of Polesden Lacey, Surrey, who was convinced that Grace Vanderbilt, one of the richest women in the world, had attempted to 'poach' her personal maid, Mademoiselle Liron. He was less amused about having to dissuade Noël Coward from attempting to offer a job and tempting incentives, including pet cats, to Nichols' own manservant, Gaskin.

# Payment and wages, tips and perks

It was customary to employ a servant for 51 weeks at a time, so that the employer could avoid the embarrassment of a sacked member of staff claiming poor relief from their parish, to which they were entitled after a year's residency and continuous employment. Senior servants were usually taken on for a longer period as they were felt to have 'proved' themselves in former positions.

Below: An agency letter requesting a character reference for Margaret Seaton applying for a situation as under housemaid (1895).

At the beginning of the nineteenth century, wages for residential servants were paid at the end of the year, the rationale being that they were housed and fed, and so needed to spend little money during their time in service. However servants often requested and received advances against their salary, so they could buy essentials such as boots and clothes, or to send money back to their families. As time passed, employers became more willing to pay in quarterly increments, and eventually monthly.

As a matter of course, female household servants were paid about half of the wages given to their male equivalents. A male chef could command as much as £120 in the 1870s, while a female cook working in a comparative kitchen received between £50 and £60. Throughout this era, women servants increasingly outnumbered men, a sign that their comparative value for money was appreciated by householders. Female staff were less costly, as they rarely required formal uniforms, unlike footmen, because they worked 'behind the scenes' and therefore wore their own clothes. No punitive tax was imposed on female staff, though householders had to pay a levy on their male employees, from the 1770s right through to the 1930s.

## MISS WRIGHT'S AGENCY,

CONDUCTED BY
[MISS J. A. WRIGHT.

DERBY HOUSE,

TELEGRAPHIC ADDRESS:
"WRIGHT'S AGENCY, STOCKTON-ON-TEES."
(THREE WORDS.)

HARTINGTON ROAD,

STOCKTON-ON-TEES,

All communications and addresses sent are strictly confidential.

Nov. 14th 1895

Re *Margaret Seaton*

Applying for situation as *Under housemaid*

MADAM,

The Servant above-mentioned has applied to me for a situation, and has referred to you for character.

I shall be much obliged if you will be so good as to inform me how long and in what capacity she was in your service; whether you found her honest, truthful, steady, industrious, respectful, and competent (mentioning any points in regard to domestic ability, commendable or otherwise, as may seem to you desirable); and whether you think she is capable of undertaking the duties of the position mentioned above, which she desires to fill.

Awaiting your esteemed reply,

I am, Madam,

Your obedient Servant,

**J. A. WRIGHT.**

## Board wages

'Board wages' were a cash supplement paid to servants remaining at their posts when the family was not in residence, so that the skeleton staff working at the house could make their own arrangements for food. Usually they would pool their resources and consequently save a sizeable sum to salt away for a rainy day.

## Tips

Tips or 'vails' were another source of income; 'blackmail in the shape of fees to servants', was how Dr Brewer described the practice of tipping in his 1897 *Dictionary of Phrase and Fable*. The custom originated in the days when peripatetic monarchs would distribute small gifts to members of a household where they had been staying. By the eighteenth century British servants were notorious throughout Europe for their flagrant attempts to squeeze money out of each departing visitor or guest.

Eventually, the ruling classes mounted a sustained campaign to stop the practice, led by George III (who was booed from the cheap seats when he visited the theatre). To reinforce the point, printed notices at Woburn Abbey in Bedfordshire asked the guests not to tip the staff, and at Mount Stewart in Northern Ireland, Lord Londonderry actively discouraged tipping of any sort. But the revolution was short-lived; servants had many subtle ways of putting a gentleman at a disadvantage if he had a reputation of being mean. Regular guests therefore made a point of tipping 'their' servants in the hope of being favoured on their next visit.

## Perks

Even hall boys had their perks. In some houses they were allowed to collect the empty wine bottles after dinner, to sell on to a dealer who gave 2d or 3d per dozen bottles. Most desirable were bottles and their matching corks from spectacular vintages; an empty port or claret bottle, complete with its authorised cork, from an excellent batch could command 5s. These were sold on to unscrupulous wine waiters in restaurants and hotels who refilled the bottle with a cheap, inferior wine, 'opened' the bottle out of the direct view of the tipsy guest and presented him with the apparently authentic wine, complete with its matching cork.

Kitchen maids were allowed to keep rabbit and hare skins – these they could sell to a travelling packman for a few pence a time, for use in glove-making. Even scullery maids were able to sell feathers, hand-plucked from ducks and geese, for making pillows and cushions.

Right: Partial view of the Scullery at Llanerchaeron. The discarded skins and feathers of game were sold by kitchen and scullery maids to supplement their wages.

Cook's 'perquisites' were often a source of friction between the mistress upstairs and the doyenne of the subterranean quarters. Traditionally, cooks had been allowed to sell off the dripping, the dark and oily residue of roasted meat, with a layer of fat on top. Dripping was sold on by dealers as a meat stock to lesser households, inns or pie-makers. Cooks anxious to provide for their old age were not above slipping the odd silver spoon into the dripping as they handed it over to the dealer, with an accompanying wink, so long as they were suitably reimbursed afterwards. Lucrative but unappealing was the collecting and selling of kitchen waste as pigswill, or the sale of old textiles and bones to rag-and-bone men, to paper mills and glue factories. In addition, cooks often negotiated a commission from local suppliers, whether in the form of an annual percentage from the local butcher, or the odd bottle of port or gin, delivered hidden under the dry goods from the favoured grocer.

In short, in most large-scale households, the employees were busily but discreetly making provision for their future lives.

# 'Invisible' servants

*...down I went at ten o'clock, walking softly across the great hall, in order not to attract the attention of those housemaids who, in large country houses, in the early hours, seem always to be lurking behind screens with the special object of shooting out of the room, when disturbed, like pheasants...*

Beverly Nichols, *All I Could Never Be*, 1949

In the grandest houses, all servants were required to blend discreetly into the background when not actually serving their betters. In some places their invisibility was absolutely essential; any servant found in one of the principal rooms might be sacked. The 3rd Lord Crewe insisted that no housemaid should ever be seen by him or any of his visitors, except at chapel, on pain of instant dismissal. The 10th Duke of Bedford also resented women servants and if he encountered any of them after midday was liable to sack them. At Canons Ashby in Northamptonshire, Sir Henry Dryden often expressed his irritation by being grumpy with the servants. When his wife, Lady Frances Dryden, gave birth to a daughter, Sir Henry stomped off in a sulk, saying 'There are too many females in this house already!' and sacking two blameless women servants unfortunate enough to cross his path. Lady Francis quietly reinstated them and the matter was never referred to again.

## Tunnels and passageways

At Uppark in Sussex, a complete complex of underground tunnels was installed in about 1815 in order to link the basement, the hub of the servants' lives, with the separate stable block, the dairy and various other estate offices, so that the servants could move around swiftly yet remain unseen by their employers. A similar arrangement was introduced at Calke Abbey in Derbyshire, the home of the reclusive and eccentric Sir Vauncey Harpur Crewe. Most of his household servants lived and worked at Calke Abbey for decades without ever meeting him.

Tunnels for the staff became very popular among those who could afford them. Cliveden was rebuilt in 1851 following a fire, and the architect Charles Barry installed a tunnel under the middle of the courtyard so that the servants could walk from one wing to another unseen by the occupants of the house. At Petworth the servants' block was a complex separate from the rest of the house, and was linked to it by a very long underground passage, with cellars to both

152

sides. Along the length of the tunnel were small niches in the walls in which candlesticks or oil lamps were placed, to provide lighting. To transport the hot food from kitchen to dining-room table before it cooled completely, servants would hurtle along the corridor bearing massive trays. Each dish would have a domed meat cover, topped with a blanket.

*It was then they'd come rushing into the kitchen with their trays, no time to waste or the food would be cold…*

Ivy Richardson, housemaid at Petworth in Sussex during the 1920s

One inevitable consequence of requiring servants to transport hot food huge distances underground from kitchen to table was the extent to which various dishes suffered in transit. Serving maids or footmen trying to carry a delicate soufflé fresh from the baking oven to the dining room 400m (¼ mile) away along an underground passageway in the depths of winter could only watch helplessly as their precious burden shrank and collapsed under the draught of

Below: Detail of the door plate to the Old Kitchen at Belton House. Keeping cooking smells out of the main house was a priority.

cold air. Enterprising footmen tried running backwards along underground tunnels carrying soufflés hidden under pre-warmed metal domes, in the forlorn hope that their cargo would arrive intact. In the morning, crisp bacon would be dispatched from the kitchen for the family's breakfast, only to be returned uneaten as it had gone soft in transit. The mistress of the house would feel obliged to complain to Cook, who would then blame the footmen, with aggrieved feelings all round.

## Keeping out of sight

As a kitchen maid at Petworth, Ivy Richardson was obliged to work behind the scenes; such humble servants rarely saw the whole house and they were not allowed to explore:

*If you worked in the kitchen you were in the kitchen and just commuted between the kitchen and your bedroom where you slept... Lord Leconfield we rarely saw. Remember the old saying that the best servants are those that are never seen. We travelled from the Servants' Block through the tunnel, never across the drive. That would have been instant dismissal...*

Of course, those who had the task of cleaning the principal rooms did at least get to see them. Harriet Best, the lowly fourth housemaid at the Sussex house recalled:

*Our instructions were that when Lord Leconfield came in [to the Marble Hall, while it was being cleaned] we all had to troop out with our buckets... when for some reason his Lordship came back into the hall... we all walked out with our buckets. Eventually he became irritated and told the housekeeper in his forthright way that he hadn't got some bloody disease. A notice was put up to this effect and after that we stayed put.*

Some householders completely ignored the servants if they unexpectedly encountered them. In less democratic times, servants had been required to turn to face the wall while their superiors passed. At Ickworth in Suffolk, the desire for servants' invisibility was taken to extremes. The layout of the house made it possible for the majority of tasks to be performed out of sight, and much of the work was done early in the morning while the family was still asleep. Firewood was left outside doors, ready for housemaids to creep in and lay and light fires before the family was awake, which must have required great stealth and dexterity. Public rooms were swept and tidied at this time, and shoes were cleaned. The 4th Marquess of Bristol believed servants should be invisible, and would bellow at any servant he met in a corridor, demanding to know what he or she was doing there. He almost never ventured 'below stairs'; a former kitchen maid recalled that in the time she worked at Ickworth, she only once caught a glimpse of him, and that was in the park.

At Penrhyn, not only were the housemaids dressed identically in black dresses with white aprons and white lace caps, they were also recruited to match each other in height. No housemaid was allowed to be in the front part of the castle after 9am. In addition all servants were expected to use the Secondary Staircase, located next to the Grand Stairs, so that staff and members of the family or their guests should not meet. At Castle Drogo in Devon, Lutyens provided a broad main staircase for the family; within the apparently solid core of the staircase, he placed a secondary, internal staircase that ran up four floors, allowing the servants to move invisibly from one part of the house to another.

Left: The utilitarian Servants' Staircase at Ham House, Richmond -upon-Thames.

# Servants' revenge

The relationship between master and servant could be extremely close, with nannies and housekeepers, butlers and valets often proving to be the best friend and confidante of their charges over decades. But sometimes servants rebelled against bad treatment from their employers; they wanted revenge.

Discretion was expected from servants, who were obliged to avert their eyes from sights 'not fit for curates', in the memorable phrase of Eric Horne, a former butler. Another butler, who worked for George Cornwallis-West, once informed his startled master that servants entertained themselves in idle moments by raiding the 'upstairs' waste-paper baskets and piecing together the fragments of torn-up letters. Inevitably, gossip was traded between servants who heard and saw more than their masters supposed, and some were able to retail these secrets in return for ready cash. The most savage sting was when servants, supposedly loyal, betrayed their position of trust. Several of Lady Colin Campbell's senior servants appeared as chief witnesses for her husband during the divorce proceedings against her, which shocked her greatly, and gave pause for thought to other unhappily married but indiscreet wives.

Below: A woman peeps through the keyhole while a journalist makes notes: 'The public wants details!' (1905).

There were occasional flashes of individual protest, such as the occasion at Dunham Massey in Cheshire when the servants went on strike after finding pieces of newspaper in their stew. There were also more subtle ways of getting even; H.G. Wells' mother was unhappily employed as a housekeeper at Uppark. He later satirised the relationship between masters and servants in his seminal novel, *The Time Machine* (1895), which contrasts the savage Morlocks, who live in Stygian gloom below ground, with the effete and ineffectual Eloi, above ground.

# Theft and burglary from employers

Servants were frequently warned to guard against any possibility of being accused of pilfering. *The Servants' Magazine* for 1856 urged:

*Be strictly honest. Some young women live with easy negligent mistresses who leave their drawers open, and even the cases in which rings and brooches, it may be necklaces and valuable trinkets, are kept, scarcely knowing what they really possess. Make it, therefore, a matter of conscience, never to take the smallest article, no, not even a piece of ribbon, however old and apparently of little worth...*

Certainly, court records of the era are full of cases in which servants were accused of theft, of clothes, jewellery and accessories, and these were probably the tip of the iceberg; to a certain extent, low-level 'skimming' was tolerated. It was understood that food in particular might be smuggled off the premises to feed dependants, and a 'blind eye' would be turned. Most theft was fairly small-time and could be viewed as 'just desserts', when a servant felt entitled to some perks from his employer. One of the many cooks employed by the long-suffering Jane Carlyle proved to be incompetent and when she left she took with her eight bottles of purloined ale.

In some households, a suspicious employer could test a new recruit's integrity by concealing a coin where he or she could find it. There were also tales of female servants who would find residential employment in wealthy houses, and then assist in a burglary by letting their villainous accomplices into the building after hours. Henry Mayhew, in his seminal work *London Labour and the London Poor* (1861) reported that these women would remain in the service of a burgled family for several months after the event in order to deflect suspicion, before moving on to their next victims.

But the ultimate revenge of servant on master was a shocking case, and gripped the nation in 1876. The estate of Dolaucothi in South Wales had been owned by the Johnes family since the sixteenth century, and was presided over by Judge John Johnes, Recorder of Carmarthen. For seventeen years he had employed a butler, Tremble, and when the position of landlord at the Dolaucothi Arms became vacant, Tremble asked if he could leave his post in service and take over the pub. Judge Johnes refused his request, because it wouldn't suit him to have to find a new butler. Tremble was devastated; he loaded a shotgun, took it to the library and murdered his employer.

# Marriage to a servant

Despite literary fancies, servants tended to marry their social equals. Indeed, close relationships between 'upstairs' and 'downstairs' were frowned upon; dedication from a servant was to be expected, as in Queen Victoria's relationship with her 'Munshi' or teacher, Abdul Karim from Agra in India, but distance should be maintained.

Victoria became very fond of Abdul Karim, and accordingly he was bitterly resented by the rest of her household. However, he did not attract the comprehensive loathing felt for his predecessor, John Brown, whom it was felt had wheedled his way into the monarch's affections; the *New York Times* even castigated the Queen for pining 'over the grave of a servant' when he died.

## Romance between employer and servant

Occasionally genuine romance blossomed between employer and servant. However, scandal could be caused when a high-born woman became involved with one of her staff; Lady Henrietta Wentworth married her footman, John William Sturgeon, and her brother, Lord Rockingham, had to endure sniggers when encouraged at his club by fellow members to 'help yourself to sturgeon'.

Sir Harry Fetherstonhaugh of Uppark surprised himself and most of polite society by falling at the advanced age of 70 for his 20-year-old dairymaid Mary Ann Bullock. He was enraptured by hearing her sing as she went about her work, and proposed marriage to the startled girl. To pre-empt a hasty reply he told her to consider the proposal and, if she consented to marriage, she should arrange for a slice to be cut out of the leg of mutton that he had ordered for dinner that night. When the joint was placed on the table, Sir Harry was delighted to see that the resourceful Mary Ann had arranged for a slice to be cut out of it.

Sir Harry initially had some misgivings; 'I've made a fool of myself, Legge', he remarked to his gamekeeper after marrying her in 1825 (sadly, Legge's response went unrecorded). The new Lady Fetherstonhaugh, *née* Bullock, was tutored at home in social niceties then dispatched to Paris for a veneer of cosmopolitanism; she was highly amused that Sir Harry apologised to her for having said 'damn' in her presence. But their marriage was a great success, and Sir Harry clung tenaciously to life until he was 90, dying in 1846. Mary Ann outlived him by nearly three decades, and on her own death in 1874 she bequeathed Uppark to her sister Frances, who adopted the family's surname, as a mark of gratitude for the implausibility of Fate.

## Social stigma

Social stigma attached itself to couples who married out of their class: Arthur Munby, the well-heeled London solicitor with a secret penchant for working women, kept his marriage to the lowly maid-of-all-work Hannah Cullwick secret, as he could not bear to tell his mother. Bizarrely, his wife seemed to accept this as natural, and also concealed their relationship.

At Dunham Massey, the seventh Earl of Stamford broke all conventional barriers in 1848 when he married Elizabeth Billage, the daughter of the man who had been his servant at Cambridge. She died in 1854, but before polite society had a chance to draw breath, the Earl married Catherine Cocks, known as 'Kitty', who was a circus-ring 'equestrienne'. 'Kitty' had a brother with a conviction for grievous bodily harm, but she was beautiful and accomplished. By comparison, marrying a servant's daughter was tame behaviour.

Below: *Jane Morris* by Dante Gabriel Rossetti, completed by Ford Madox Brown. 'Janey', as she was known, came from humble origins before her marriage to William Morris.

Marrying out of one's class did bring practical drawbacks. William Morris was smitten by Jane Burden, the 17-year-old daughter of an Oxford stableman and his illiterate wife. 'Janey' was intelligent and beautiful, but barely educated; without her burgeoning career as an artist's model and the infatuation of Morris, she would almost certainly have gone into domestic service. Morris, a gentleman from a well-to-do family, had a comfortable income of £900 a year. On their engagement, he paid for Janey to receive a private education to fit her for life as his wife; she became an avid reader and showed a flair for foreign languages. However, she was ill at ease directing their servants, never having done so before.

# Servants' balls

In the mid-Victorian era, the trend grew for large households to hold occasional parties for their servants, as it was felt that loyalty from the staff should be rewarded. Mistresses were advised to make it very clear that they were in charge, by choosing a day when the master of the house was away so that he could not be inconvenienced, and ensuring temperance and modest behaviour in the revellers.

Each servant would be allowed one guest each, and male guests must be either a relative or a recognised suitor. Tea and cakes were provided, and decorous games and pursuits were encouraged, even a little dancing. The whole event should be concluded by 10pm, when the servants had to restore the room to its usual state and depart, presumably suitably appreciative of their mistress's *largesse*.

Aristocratic families often put on parties for their staff, and usually attended themselves. In January 1902, the Robartes family of Lanhydrock organised a celebration for their staff and tenants, to celebrate the 21st birthday of their eldest son, Tommy. A well-attended foxhunt was followed by tea for the servants and tenants, in a large marquee, which had been erected in the courtyard. The trestle tables were laden with food and were decorated for a huge feast, and there were speeches and toasts. In addition, a 'moving picture show' was put on in the servants' hall.

Conversation at these events could be a little stilted, but the good intentions of the family were usually evident, and appreciated; a band would be brought in, so there would be dancing, and battalions of temporary staff cooked and served the food and drink, which was a great treat for the house servants. The outdoor servants were usually also included, a chance for match-making between domestic and estate workers.

Some households regularly held social events for their staff. Every Friday evening there was a social club in the servants' quarters at Polesden Lacey with a bar, music and a billiard table. At Penrhyn Castle in the early 1900s, Annie Evans recalled, 'The butler, Mr Sharpe, was a good man. He was a teetotaller, but he loved dancing and there were dances in the steward's room every month, with a band from Bangor. The staff were contented.' Other servants felt

Right: *Haste to the Wedding* by Phyllis Sandeman at Lyme Park, Cheshire.

that 'a bit of fun' was good for staff morale; it was an opportunity
for young people in particular to let off steam, and many of them
took up musical instruments so that they could put together a house
band for dancing.

It is apparent from contemporary accounts that at these events the
servants saw each other in a new light; it was a rare opportunity to
see one's familiar colleagues as they might have been if life had
been different:

*It was quite a revelation to see all of the members of the staff in ball dress.
Even the prim head housemaid looked quite chic in a velvet gown, and was
almost unrecognisable without her stiff, black silk dress and her belt of jingling
keys. Many members of staff looked so well in their ball clothes that it sparked
off the party; and, as I looked around, I found that we had acquired a new
kind of individuality and gaiety for the evening and, stranger still, that we
were seeing each other from a new aspect – as people, not servants.*

Frederick Gorst, *Of Carriages and Kings*, 1956

# Free time for servants

Above: Detail of a parlour game (Halma, a version of chequers, invented in Britain around 1880) in the Drawing Room at Sunnycroft in Shropshire.

## Spare time during the day

Despite the long hours, there were various natural breaks in the day when most household servants could relax and catch their breath. For the butler, it might be the interval between lunch and tea when he could slip out to a pub, if in town, or 'catch up on his accounts' in his sitting room, usually a euphemism for a snooze. Cooks were similarly glad of a chance to put their feet up maybe with a book, a magazine or a welcome visitor, leaving the provision of tea for 'upstairs' to the lesser staff. Needlework and reading were considered worthwhile occupations for female staff; they looked busy, even if it was ultimately an opportunity to sit down and relax.

With luck, a well-provisioned servants' hall might be fitted with comfortable seats, even a sofa, and some forms of entertainment. A few enlightened employers provided a few board games, such as 'Halma', or even a piano. But this was unusual – most servants were thrown back on their own resources to find entertainment, and would eke out their few free hours in a minimally furnished communal hall, nearly always in the basement, where they were expected to keep an eye on the bellboard. Inevitably, this ill-assorted company, crammed together below stairs in conditions that were less than comfortable, would get on each other's nerves.

## Fun in the evenings

Music-making was a welcome means of breaking the monotony. At Ickworth in Suffolk, when the family were away, the kitchen staff would join the housemaids, footmen and hall boys for a musical evening – one would play the piano and the rest would sing. More formalised opportunities for enjoyment were welcome. At Powis Castle the 29 indoor servants were allowed a dance in the servants' hall every Friday evening, and two of the outdoor staff would come in to play the fiddle for the residents. As the kitchen maid recalled, 'This was our only entertainment as nobody had any time off during the week. Half the staff had a few hours one Sunday and the other half the following Sunday.'

## Opportunities for sport and learning

Male staff at large houses often formed a football or cricket team. At Petworth in Sussex, the business of cricket was taken so seriously that Lord Egremont employed a professional cricketer to coach the team, drawn from the 24 grooms and coachmen, the 25 gardeners, the estate workers and indoor menservants.

Benign employers made a great difference to how servants chose to spend their leisure; some actually put together a lending library of improving literature specifically for their servants, such as that at Polesden Lacey. At Uppark in West Sussex the young H.G. Wells educated himself by plundering the household library.

## The bicycle

Getting out of doors was the best break of all, and the invention of the bicycle revolutionised the quality of servants' leisure time. Throughout the 1890s bicycling became increasingly popular. A fit young man could cover perhaps 6.5km (4 miles) an hour at a steady walk, but in the same time he could be 24 or 32km (15 or 20 miles) away if he had a bicycle.

At Ickworth at the turn of the century, all the younger servants, whose families lived close enough, went home whenever they had the opportunity. They had a half day off every week, and every other Sunday they were allowed to leave after lunch (the scullery maid had to stay until she had done the washing up), returning by 10pm. Most had bicycles, and had to ride at least an hour each way. A bicycle was a big financial investment but it could be purchased by instalments, and the independence it gave young women in particular was remarkable. Even the not-so-young were able to cycle: the German governess at Lyme Park, Fraulein Thür, small, round and elderly though she was, was a cycling enthusiast.

Below: The uneven surfaces of rural roads, and the instability of the bicycle, were, alas, apt to cause occasional regrettable mishaps such as this (c.1870).

# Sundays in service

In the mid-Victorian era, the notion of Sunday being a 'day of rest' was taken very seriously by many. Parks and museums were shut, concerts and 'frivolous' music were banned, and reading 'worldly' texts, such as newspapers or novels, was discouraged.

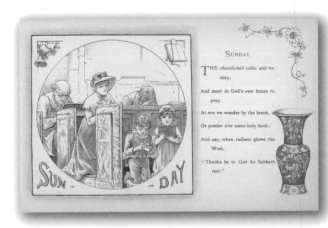

Above: *Churchgoers* (1886). On Sundays the housemaid and others go to church on their day of rest.

*Let us, therefore, ever remember that the duties of our respective stations are appointed by our heavenly Father, and must be fulfilled according to His will.*

Editorial from *The Servants' Magazine*, January 1856

Numerous Christian sects specifically forbade a wide range of everyday activities on Sundays. Consequently, any family with a reputation for devoutness, tended to devote their Sundays to attendance at religious services in their own chapel, good works such as visiting the sick, or the reading of improving tracts.

Some families would ride in their landau or carriage to church, while the more pious would walk so that their grooms and coachmen could also attend the service. The family would occupy one of the best pews; their servants, wearing their Sunday clothes, would walk as a group to the same church, but sit quietly at the back of the nave. Many of them enjoyed the excursion; it was a rare opportunity to get some exercise in the fresh air and to gaze at and speculate about the villagers in the congregation – people who were neither their colleagues nor their bosses. For an hour or so every week, they could sit and think their own thoughts, free from the demands of ringing bells or peremptory orders. They might even have a free afternoon to look forward to, to be spent with friends or family, once they had completed the clearing up after lunch.

# Holidays for servants

Apart from the odd half day's holiday, throughout the nineteenth century the opportunities for servants to enjoy extended free time were limited. Holiday arrangements depended on one's employer. The most generous offered a fortnight's holiday a year, along with a half day every Sunday, a whole day at leisure per month, and one evening of free time a week. Individual days off were a boon for those who wished to visit their families, so long as their homes were accessible. But for those who went into service at the turn of the century, such as the droves of maids from Scotland and Wales employed by wealthy London families, their opportunities to return home were limited to once or twice a year, as a return day trip was impossible.

Of course, many would have seen a whole fortnight's holiday as an unimaginable luxury – Mrs Beeton in her *Domestic Service Guide* (1875) expressed her view that in the country a servant might expect a week per year, but that in service in London there could be no guarantee of a holiday and a servant would be lucky to be rewarded with a free day perhaps once every six weeks. The issue of holidays was ultimately an important factor in the gradual drift from residential domestic service to salaried work in mills and factories, department stores and offices, where hours of working were well-defined and one's free time could not be eroded by the constant demands of an insatiable household.

Above: *Out for a Holiday* (1849) by George Cruikshank.

# Ill servants

Life in service was physically hard for the lower servants, and they often aged prematurely from a life of unremitting toil, poor medical care and very long hours. A housemaid typically worked a 16-hour day, at least six-and-a-half days a week, while her sister in a factory was more likely to work a 12-hour shift with a half day on Saturdays and a 'day of rest' on Sundays.

## Care for ill servants

When a senior servant stayed with a single family for most of his or her working life, there was felt to be a moral obligation on the part of the employer to provide for them if they fell ill. However, this was not universally observed; indeed Mrs Beeton, whose readership was predominantly middle class, held that the mistress was under no obligation to care for an ill servant if it appeared that the sickness might incapacitate him or her permanently.

Some employers were extremely loyal to their servants in illness, regardless of their comparatively humble status. At Lanhydrock, the Robartes family summoned a doctor whenever one of the servants was ill. Florence Nightingale often expressed concern about the health of her servants, and she supported the parents of her maid, Lizzie Coleman, when they fell ill, covering additional medical costs.

Below: The medicine cabinet at Dunster Castle in Somerset, showing jars containing lavender, calomela, Rochell Salts, caster oil, laudanum and Dr James's fever powder.

## Medicines

Servants often relied on patent medicines for self-treatment; these were easy to acquire but often contained ingredients that merely masked pain and could not tackle the underlying symptoms. J. Collis Browne's Chlorodyne was marketed as an effective remedy against coughs, stomach cramps, diarrhoea and sleeplessness – hardly surprising, as it contained chloral hydrate, cannabis and opium.

Home remedies abounded through the nineteenth century and were collected and used by servants. 'My Mother's Note-book' was a regular column in *The Servants' Magazine*, and the columnist thought highly of the medicinal qualities of bacon. In the case of a 'Common Sore Throat, however severe', the sufferer was advised to fry some bacon and while it was still hot, to apply the rasher to the affected part of the neck, before wrapping the throat in flannel to hold the bacon in place and going to bed.

## Healthcare before the welfare state

Before the coming of the welfare state, healthcare for the poor and working classes was patchy, and had to be paid for by the individual, their family, a sponsor such as an employer, or a charity. Hospitals did exist, usually set up as charitable institutions supported by the better-off; in rural areas, there might be cottage hospitals, which varied in competence but provided basic medical care. In cities, particular hospitals became known for treating specific conditions, and others were distinguished by the classes they served: St George's Hospital at Hyde Park Corner in London was well known for treating gentlemen's servants for all sorts of ailments, and it relied upon donations from the gentry for its income.

For those ill servants who fell through the net, there were infirmaries attached to workhouses, though these were bleak places and avoided if there were any alternative. The workhouse being the 'end of the line', respectable former servants whose entire working life had been erected on a pyramid of social hierarchy would shudder at the thought of sharing a communal ward with the detritus of society, the confused, the feckless and the unfortunate.

*...the health of servants is really better, on the whole, than that of their ladies... a lady who has been teaching and watching over her children, or who has been occupied in mind with her husband's affairs, may well be more fatigued than the housemaid who has been scouring her rooms...*

*The Nursery Maid: Her Duties and How to Perform Them*, Houlton's Industrial Library, 1877

Above: Woolley's Ltd Chemists Chlorodyne Lozenges bottle label (1908).

# The National Insurance Act

It was apparent that some provision needed to be made for the care of the elderly and ill servants. In 1911 the Liberal government, led by David Lloyd George, proposed a bill that would provide free medical treatment and benefit payments during illness. Each employer would pay 3d per week in tax for a female servant, and 4d a week for a manservant, matched by an equal amount from each servant themselves.

The provision of insurance supported the servant in the event of sickness or unemployment. While eligible, medical bills would be covered and for six months the female servant could claim 7/6d per week, while her male colleague would get 10 shillings a week in benefits. This was hardly a fortune but it would maintain them at subsistence level. If permanently incapacitated by illness, they could claim a very small pension of 5 shillings a week.

This innovation was met with suspicion by many householders and servants alike, fuelled by some inflammatory editorials from the *Daily Mail*, which felt that it would destroy the 'bond of trust' between mistress and servant. Of course, in households in which the family was benign and generous, any servant unfortunate enough to fall ill would be cared for. It was those households in which servants were considered dispensable that the problems arose. It is likely also that wealthy families resented the implication that they were shirking in their charitable duties; in more modest establishments, the 'tax' on each servant to be paid by the employer and the necessary rise in each servant's wages to meet their share of the bill had a negative effect on carefully managed budgets. Despite a concerted letter-writing campaign, and a call to a protest meeting at the Royal Albert Hall led by the Dowager Lady Desart, Lloyd George disarmed the opposition and the bill passed into law in 1912.

Below: *Insurance Stamps* (1911), a cartoon satirising Lloyd George's National Insurance Act.

AM I SUPPOSED TO STICK THE STAMPS ON MYSELF?

INSURANCE ACTS

# Old age

Senior servants in large households, once relieved of the more physically arduous tasks through promotion, often lasted to a ripe old age, particularly compared with their peers in the outside world. Cooks worked on into their sixties, septuagenarian nannies were not unknown, and ancient butlers were often kept on as long as they could still carry a tray.

The average life expectancy of a man in the mid-nineteenth century was 41, and that of a woman 44, but in the newly industrialised cities, many of the working classes died in their twenties, worn out by endless shifts of grinding, dangerous labour in factories, mills and mines, or wiped out by disease. The life of junior domestic servants was physically demanding, but they were provided with heat and light, decent clothing, warmth and ample food, and could usually depend on remaining secure in their posts so long as they fulfilled their duties. With few outgoings, and the occasional tips or perks, it was also possible for a frugal servant to accrue a decent sum to provide for his or her old age.

Below: Engraving in *The British Workman* (1862) In 1861 the Palmerston government set up the Post Office Savings Bank encouraging ordinary wage earners to provide for themselves against adversity and ill health.

## Savings

In an era before state pensions, wise servants attempted to save most of their wages. In 1861 the Post Office introduced the concept of savings banks, and young servants were encouraged to buy stamps for their account books. The interest rates were unspectacular – 6d per annum for each full sovereign saved – but the books could be redeemed for cash when required. Responsible mistresses encouraged thrift in their staff, seeing this as a virtue for its own sake as well as a hedge against a possibly lengthy and poverty-ridden old age. Some servants asked their employers to invest their nest eggs on their behalf. Publications aimed at servants echoed the same message with a combination of religious maxims and practical advice:

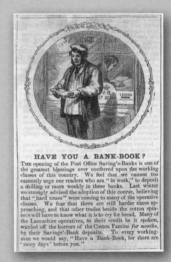

**HAVE YOU A BANK-BOOK?**
The opening of the Post Office Saving's-Banks is one of the greatest blessings ever conferred upon the working classes of this country. We feel that we cannot too earnestly urge our readers who are "in work," to deposit a shilling or more weekly in these banks. Last winter we strongly advised the adoption of this course, believing that "hard times" were coming to many of the operative classes. We fear that there are still harder times approaching, and that other trades beside the cotton spinners will have to know what it is to cry for bread. Many of the Lancashire operatives, to their credit be it spoken, warded off the horrors of the Cotton Famine *for months*, by their Savings'-Bank deposits. To every working-man we would say, "Have a Bank-Book, for there are 'rainy days' before you."

*…Calculate your income and, if possible, do not let your expenses be more than three quarters of it. Thus if you earn ten shillings weekly, put by half-a-crown. Some young people will be ready to say this is impossible. By no means, it is only acting as though you did not earn more than seven shillings and sixpence a week.*

*The Servants' Magazine*, April 1856

Savings were the servants' obsession; their passport to a life after service, or a provision for their old age. One late nineteenth-century former housekeeper at Erddig managed to save £1,300 (£77,857 in today's values), an impressive sum.

## Noblesse oblige

On the death of an employer, there were often provisions in the master's or mistress's will to assist the servant's transition to the next job, or to care for him or her in retirement. Long-serving staff frequently received a lump sum in recognition of their devoted service. Some were pensioned off by 'their' families, with a decent annuity, enough to live comfortably (if modestly) to the end of their days. Landed families felt a genuine sense of '*noblesse oblige*' to their dependents. Some estates, such as Saltram in Devon, had cottages built on their land to provide accommodation for former servants. Where the retiring servant had a family, he or she would often move in with them, supported by a pension from the former employer.

## Charity and almshouses

For those less fortunate in their old age, a few places offered refuge. The Servants' Benevolent Institution was set up in 1846 by a former servant, William Ashwell, relying on charity from the wealthy to provide almshouses and pensions for retired servants. It also made small payments to those attempting to recover from illness. Those without families and few means of support would be lucky to find a place in an almshouse, as demand far outstripped supply. Hard-pressed applicants had to convince the governors that they were in genuine need, and of excellent character, in order to gain a place. *The Servants' Magazine* of 1857 published what purported to be a letter from 'An Aged Servant':

*…How nice it would be if there could be a comfortable dwelling for all servants that are past labour and have but little to live on. Alms-houses are so very difficult to get into. I think there are a very few in London for servants, but I do not know of any in country-places. I was thinking if gentlemen that have waste land would build cottages and let them to servants for a small rent, it would be a great comfort to them… there are some rich families that provide for their servants when they are past duty; and there are many kind and good masters and mistresses that would gladly do so if they could, who find it hard to part with an old servant's past labour… I am a plain servant, and have not the understanding to know how or who to apply to, and I know your little magazine finds its way to the drawing-room of many rich families…*

# The workhouse

In an era before the welfare state, the poor, ill and vulnerable might call first upon their former employers, then the comfort of strangers through the *ad hoc* provision of charity. When these failed them, they resorted to the workhouse.

## The Poor Laws

Until the 1908 Poor Law was passed, the workhouse was virtually the last resort for Victorian and Edwardian servants who had fallen on hard times, through bad luck, illness or old age. This much-feared institution was a source of dread and shame for the respectable working classes, and a much-resented imposition on the more louche members of society. At the turn of the century it was estimated that about one in 20 of the population aged 65 or over was a resident in a workhouse.

Beginning in 1834, a network of workhouses was created, modelled on the experimental workhouse at Southwell in Nottinghamshire. Poverty had always existed, and many people lived hand-to-mouth, perhaps with some support from their parish, or benefactors. Those who had not saved during their working lives, or were unlucky enough to have lost their fortunes and families, faced a bleak future. The workhouse systematised the provision of assistance, so that paupers would have access to a competently administered but dismally dour institution where they could be fed, clothed, housed and given some form of elementary occupation.

Above: Anti-Poor Law poster (c.1834) showing the interior of an English workhouse under the new laws.

## The 'deserving' poor

There were many categories of 'pauper' who found their way to the workhouse. They were divided into two types, the 'deserving' and the 'undeserving' poor. The first category had fallen on hard times through no fault of their own. A typical story was that of Mary Beer from Cornwall: when she was a child her father died, and her destitute mother and siblings had no choice but to go to the workhouse. As a horse and cart was taking them away, one of the daughters from Cotehele in Cornwall chose Mary as the prettiest of the children, to be taken on and trained as a servant at the Big House. The family was therefore separated, but Mary was provided with a means of making a living.

Sadly, there were also many others who were merely too elderly or frail to cope on their own; widows and widowers, if they had no other relatives, might well end their days in the workhouse. Former servants who were unlucky or penniless, or incapacitated by arthritis or rheumatism, heart conditions or bronchitis, often entered the workhouse and spend their last years in its hospital wards.

In 1908 the Old Age Pension Act was brought in 'to lift the shadow of the workhouse from the homes of the poor', as Lloyd George put it. Under the terms of the new law, a person aged 70 or over and in receipt of less than 12 shillings a week was entitled to a modest state pension. Nevertheless, the grim prospect of ending one's days as a pauper in the workhouse remained a genuine concern to all servants.

*Perhaps one in a hundred butlers gets a sort of pension, enough to keep him out of the workhouse… if I must die in the workhouse, I must.*

Eric Horne, *What the Butler Winked At*, 1924

## The 'undeserving' poor

By contrast, the 'undeserving poor' included those who appeared to be fit and healthy but were deemed unwilling to work at some respectable trade. Vagrants, itinerant labourers and former soldiers and sailors came into this category. Those thought to have brought their misfortune on themselves, such as prostitutes and unmarried mothers, as well as servants rendered unemployable because they had been turned out by previous employers without a character reference, fell into this category, and were treated accordingly by the Master and Matron of the workhouse. Grim though the regime was, staying in the workhouse was not compulsory; adult inmates could be discharged, if they gave a short period of notice to the Master, but they had to take their dependants with them. This was to avoid feckless parents dumping their unwanted offspring 'on the parish'.

Some orphaned children were sent to work as trainee servants in nearby grand houses, but this experimental act of benevolence on the part of a wealthy employer was rarely successful. The workhouse children were typically so starved of visual and mental stimulus that they had became institutionalised at a young age; they lacked language skills, and usually did not know the names or purposes of common household articles. They tended to find the hustle and bustle of Victorian homes incomprehensible. Even worse, they were often resented by the regular servants who disliked them on the credible grounds that they might be lousy or diseased, and the less credible ones that these children were the products of sin, and that bad luck might be contagious.

Above: The Workhouse, Southwell, Nottinghamshire. The workhouse was designed by William A. Nicholson and opened in 1824 as the prototype for all subsequent workhouses in Britain.

# 6 THE BEGINNING OF THE END

## Why it all ended

Many of the historic houses we now visit, which are clean and well lit, with ample lighting, central heating and efficient plumbing, would have been uncomfortable and impractical places in which to work.

However, the house itself might be a magnificent mansion set in rolling acres of carefully contrived 'natural' beauty, and the family might live in considerable elegance, occupying well-proportioned, exquisitely decorated principal rooms, opulently furnished and hung with magnificent works of art. By contrast, resident servants found their quarters too hot or too cold, dimly lit, dirty, malodorous and unhealthy. 'Upstairs' might be grand and ornate, but the servant's role was merely to maintain such grandeur, not to feel part of it. The staff worked in daylight hours in their own quarters and at night-time were confined under the eaves or above the stables. They had very little leisure and almost nowhere else to go in their limited time off. Forced to live cheek by jowl as part of a rigid hierarchy, they easily became discontent.

Employers and employees had differing expectations. The Victorian and Edwardian upper classes expected their orders to be obeyed. There was a general belief in meritocracy, underpinned by the social order, tempered with a sense of *noblesse oblige* – the knowledge that privilege brought its own duties. Landed families generally believed in God and the monarchy and the imposition of swift but fair punishment for transgressors.

### Christian values and social change

One factor which profoundly affected the relationship between master and servant at this time was the prevailing Christian ideology. Most people of any social standing paid lip service at least to the Church of England. Many were, indeed, genuinely devout and struggled to apply the philanthropic teachings of the New

Right: The Erddig Prayer, found in the corridor, below some of the servants' bells at Erddig, Wales.

Testament to their own perception of the vast gulf between rich and poor. Regarding servants, the prevailing belief was that God had defined each person's place in society, so one should not attempt to upset the *status quo*. But the Evangelical Movement urged people to live by example and to support charitable causes and also to be more tolerant and forbearing in their own behaviour. Gradually these ideas percolated through society and led to better treatment of servants and the lower orders.

Social change was evident around the turn of the century; mass communications, such as newspapers, photography and magazines, allowed new ideas about the world to spread. The sacred institution of live-in servants was to suffer under competition from more attractive options. Those choices – to work on the railways, in factories, mills, offices or shops – had two great advantages: regulated hours of employment, followed by free time. Domestic service provided respectability, and a certainty about one's place in the social hierarchy. For some it offered a ready-made social life, a chance even to travel, plenty of food, a roof over one's head and wages that one had no time to spend. But that was the essence of the problem; constantly on call to meet the various demands of one's employers, watched by other servants, with few holidays or opportunities to meet one's social equals, those contemplating a life in service recognised that they would have perpetual responsibility without power. At the whim of a virtual stranger, servants could be dismissed without a reference; there was no overtime for working extra hours; and to achieve promotion they would either have to wait for a colleague to retire or die, or constantly move from one grand house to the next, chasing promotion. Then there was the issue of relationships: romantic involvements were discouraged, and female servants were usually dismissed on marriage. Menservants were often refused permission to marry, as the householder wanted them available at all hours of the day or night. By the beginning of the twentieth century young people were becoming resistant to constraint or scrutiny from their social superiors.

*The rich man in his castle,*
*The poor man at his gate,*
*God made them high or lowly,*
*And ordered their estate…*

Cecil Frances Alexander, 'All Things Bright and Beautiful', 1848

MAY HEAV'N PROTECT OUR HOME FROM FLAME,
OR HURT OR HARM OF VARIOUS NAME!
AND MAY NO EVIL LUCK BETIDE
TO ANY WHO THEREIN ABIDE!
AS ALSO WHO THEIR HOMES HAVE FOUND
ON ANY ACRE OF IT'S GROUND,
OR WHO FROM HOMES BEYOND IT'S GATE
BESTOW THEIR TOIL ON THIS ESTATE!

—P Y

# New technology and a new world

New technology made supernumerary servants redundant. The motor car allowed people to travel great distances in relative comfort and little time, but it also transformed the domestic economy. Delivery vans could bring to one's door an order transmitted by telephone. Commercial laundries collected and delivered the linen. Central heating and electric lighting were cleaner and more efficient than coal fires and gas lamps. The vacuum cleaner revolutionised the arduous drudgery associated with carpets. In essence, fewer servants were required in any house with pretensions to modernism.

Servants' wages also became more expensive, and the wealthy were starting to feel the squeeze. Income tax rose inexorably, and the innovation of death duties in 1894, and their subsequent increase in 1909 and 1919, took a further toll on families who had previously been able to maintain a household of staff. Some landowners were realistic about the future: Lord Newton, of Lyme Park in Cheshire, told his daughter that country houses like theirs were an 'incubus' and that it was more realistic to move to a villa by the sea (which

Right: One of the servants' bedroom at Lanhydrock. Comfortably furnished, with a carpet, armchair and footstool, this room was a haven to a servant in the late nineteenth century.

horrified Lady Newton). He predicted that before long such a way of life would become a necessity for landed families caring for huge, expensive, anachronistic estates.

But there was a contrasting point of view: in her novel, *The Edwardians* (1930), Vita Sackville-West wrote about the various inhabitants of a magnificent country house, Chevron. She portrayed the real 'owners' of the house as the senior servants, who had lived there all their adult lives; they had an entire social edifice to maintain, with battlements of hierarchies and buttresses of tradition. To Vita Sackville-West, whose gender prevented her from inheriting her beloved ancestral home, Knole, the landowning aristocratic family existed in order to support the servants and their families, their customs and their status. *Noblesse oblige* indeed.

The 1914–18 war finally put paid to the unquestioning reliance on domestic service for all but very wealthy households. Grand houses were forced to close up most of their rooms and struggle on with a reduced workforce. When the Armistice was finally sounded and the young men started to return to a 'Land Fit For Heroes', many of them resisted returning to the old order of deference and division.

*When we came back and saw all that at Lyme, we thought what'd we been fighting for?*

Jack Leech, First World War veteran, on his return to Lyme Park, quoted by Kedrun Laurie in *Cricketer Preferred: Estate workers at Lyme Park, 1898–1946*, 1979

'Life in service' changed beyond all recognition in the space of less than 80 years. From the accession of Queen Victoria in 1837, to the shocking carnage of the Great War, the system of supporting the landowning classes in return for bed, board and a small salary underwent a gradual revolution. During those years, the British landscape was seamed with new railways, canals and viaducts; small, sleepy agricultural communities found themselves the centres of rapidly metastasising industrial cities, dotted with mills, factories and mines. The mass-produced fruits of these labours were sold overseas in the burgeoning markets of the greatest trading empire since Roman times. The revenue generated by trade was harnessed by the entrepreneurs and inventors, the financiers, traders and bankers, to forge an *élite* distinct from those of the ancestral landowning classes. They could buy land and engage an architect, or snap up an historic estate. Whatever their grand designs, householders needed servants to make them work. And when servants were at a premium, technology filled the breach.

# The shortage of servants

By the beginning of the twentieth century, there was a growing sense of unease over what was known as the 'Servant Problem'. While senior servants appeared as trustworthy as before, employers in all but the grandest houses were becoming aware that there had been a sea change among their younger staff. No longer were housemaids, boot boys and scullery maids automatically submissive and deferential. Some blamed the introduction of compulsory education for the lower orders at Board Schools, and secretly suspected that their teachers were stirring up socialist inclinations.

## Other options

In truth, there were many factors contributing to the fundamental change of attitude to domestic service. The provision of universal state education made the working classes realise that their children's lives need not be bound by the limitations imposed on their parents, through the simple expedient of literacy and numeracy. There were more options for a bright and personable teenager; a boy might

scrape a first job as an office messenger, progressing to become a clerical junior, and eventually a clerk. By learning to operate a typewriter, he could get promoted to the position of stenographer. Working for the postal and telegraph service provided a decent living and regular, well-defined hours. For the less literate but more self-reliant and physically active, 'going on the railways', as a guard or station master attracted men who had a mechanical and practical frame of mind. Meanwhile the ever-expanding shipyards, steelworks and coal mines needed clerks and assessors, sales agents and secretaries, as well as the labourers engaged to turn out the product.

## Women and social change

For women, the social changes were even more profound. To a certain extent, an individual's future career depended on where she was living when opportunity knocked. In the booming textile towns of Lancashire, there were always ways of making a living in the industrialised factories and mills. The wages were never lavish, but there were advantages: the factory girl gained independence from the constant scrutiny of an employer, and a certain amount of autonomy. Humdrum shiftwork, even for ten hours a day, while left largely to one's own thoughts (albeit against a noisy background), was the factory girl's workaday experience. Regular hours were balanced with evenings and Saturday afternoons free of commitments, and the inviting prospect of a social life spent with people of one's own class, background and experience. As architect J.J. Stevenson remarked in 1880:

*In shops and warehouses they may have harder work and longer hours, less wages, worse food, and worse rooms, but they have some time they can call their own every day.*

J.J. Stevenson, *Household Architecture*, vol II, 1880

By comparison, the mill girl's social equal, the housemaid, would work fifteen or sixteen hours a day, beginning before dawn by creeping around the sleeping household in silence, so as to lay and light fires in six or eight grates before anyone else woke up, and hiding herself if an employer hoved into view, even turning to face the corridor wall, pretending to be invisible, if cornered.

Girls contemplating a life in service began to consider their fate: did they really want to be stuck seven days a week in some archaic rural backwater, ekeing out each day's repetitive drudgery as a lowly cog in a caste-ridden miniature court? J.J. Stevenson succinctly identified the problem in 1880:

*In old days when there were no railways, a country girl taken as a servant in a great house had the best chance she could hope for in life. Now the facilities of communication give opportunity to all to move about and better themselves. Numberless employments are now open to young women, in mills and shops and warehouses, and even in counting-houses, and the Post Office gives employment to a large number in telegraph and other offices throughout the country.*

The advent of mass-transport systems allowed people to move in search of a better job, more congenial surroundings and a wider gene pool. The railways revolutionised the pursuit of work almost as greatly as the advance of literacy. Despite the agricultural depression of the 1880s, for country-dwellers, going to work at the Big House, following in one's ancestors' footsteps, was no longer automatic. Bright young women from the lower classes started to consider their increasingly numerous options.

### Other opportunities

There were ample opportunities in shop work, serving in one of the new department stores, and specialist drapers, milliners and glove-makers were opening in the big cities. These enterprises deliberately recruited former servants, those who had a feel for fashion, and were tactful with the customers. For women with a sense of vocation, Florence Nightingale had reclaimed the profession of nursing after the horrors of the Crimean campaign, establishing it as a respectable and honourable way for a bright and hard-working young woman to make a living. And, of course, there was the example of the Board School teacher herself, a noble and rewarding occupation that produced tangible results, namely successive waves of children being able to read and write.

# Emigration

The Empire was a source of great national pride; vast swathes of the globe were coloured pink, and were administered by motivated and resourceful Britons who required servants for specific roles in their expatriate homes. British nannies, governesses and even (for the homesick) traditional cooks were remunerated handsomely. For experienced and resourceful servants who wanted to travel, here was a long-awaited opportunity for subsidised adventure and a decent salary.

## Opportunities in the colonies

The colonial settlers of Canada, Australia, New Zealand and South Africa were clamouring for domestic servants, and the British government devised support schemes to send 'surplus' working-class women out to these new settlements. In certain cases, individual parishes clubbed together to despatch an unemployed family to the New World, both as a philanthropic gesture to give them a fresh start, and to reduce the expenditure on the local workhouse. The one-way ticket to Australasia in the 1880s cost approximately £3 (£145 today) per adult, with £2 (£95 today) expenses for food. It took resilience to endure the journey, but a maid or governess could earn three times the amount she could expect at home, and in a society where women were scarce, she stood a better chance of marrying a householder or landowner.

## The lure of America

North America was the first choice of would-be emigrants because of the stigma of Australia's former role as a penal colony. To many, America seemed like a land of golden opportunity. There was a new class of American entrepreneurs who had made millions in transcontinental railroads or Chicago stockyards, steel mills or newspapers. They were willing to pay handsomely for experienced British butlers, and Scottish nannies who had previously changed the nappies of infant dukes. The American regard for British servants at this time was not inverted snobbery: successful businessmen were adept at identifying the best staff for all their ventures, and they applied the same criteria in finding household staff.

Below: White Star Line poster advertising travel on the world's largest liner between Southampton and New York.

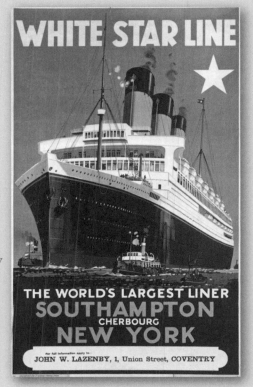

# 'Ladies' helps'– alternative servants

Back in Britain, those who kept servants were often resistant to change. Mistresses complained about the gradual rise in servants' wages, yet still expected their lady's maid to wait up until the small hours so as to help them undress. 'Followers' were discouraged, which gave a female servant almost no opportunity to court, marry and escape from servitude.

Some mistresses would expect the housemaid to bathe their lapdogs, and clean their WCs to a pearly finish every day, yet would provide nothing more hygienic than a chipped ewer, an ancient bowl, and an enamel 'gazunder' chamber pot, in the servant's sparsely furnished attic room. Why would any servant choose to remain in service?

## Ladies' helps

In the 1890s, it was argued in the press, particularly *The Spectator*, that there were many 'gentlewomen' of straitened circumstances who might be 'willing to assist' in superior households in return for a salary, so long as they were not asked to undertake anything distasteful. Where it was tried, the 'ladies' helps' experiment was usually an unmitigated failure. A workmate who spoke like the mistress and was too refined to light a fire, too delicate to scrub a floor, unable to carry gallons of hot water up endless flight of stairs, and unwilling to eat a hearty meal at the same table, was bound to cause friction. In a few cases, 'ladies helps' were a boon, usually acting as a genteel 'paid companion' to some pleasant elderly widow, a congenial arrangement that suited both parties, but as a long-term solution to the national shortage of domestic labour, it was not a success.

## Freelance servants – the 'daily'

By the beginning of the twentieth century, the cities were full of older women, often former servants, who would offer their services on a freelance basis, as 'charwomen' or 'to do the rough', maybe helping out in the kitchen when there was a large dinner party, or assisting in major spring cleans when the family were away. These women now lived independently and were prepared to work designated hours for an agreed rate of pay. With the increasing shortage of servants and a subsequent rise in their wages and living costs, there was a growing market for reliable 'charwomen' or 'dailies', and they could earn a respectable living.

## The erosion of deference

The drift away from a professional life of deference, long hours and drudgery was an inevitable consequence of the lure of other job opportunities.

*Wood must be cut and carried, hot-water bottles put into beds, inkstands filled, breakfast trays prepared, blinds raised or lowered; housemaids must vanish silently if surprised at their tasks, hall-boys must not be allowed to whistle, Vigeon [the Butler] must wear London clothes in the country, no noise must be made anywhere lest her Grace should hear it and be annoyed… in a word, life for the great and wealthy must be made as pleasant as possible.*

Vita Sackville-West, *The Edwardians*, 1930

For the wealthy, it was still possible to find reliable domestic servants, even if the rise in the annual wages bill and the National Insurance paid per employee was an irritation. Many landowners planned for the future assuming an endless supply of willing domestic labour. In 1911, at Castle Drogo, Edwin Lutyens and his client, Julius Drewe, had been thrilled by their gigantic *folie à deux*. Technologically advanced though it was in many ways, Castle Drogo was already an anachronism even as it was being built. Furthermore, neither architect nor client could have foreseen that within three years the very workforce on whom the whole edifice depended would be dodging bullets and drowning in mud in the trenches.

Left: Photograph of Annie Gerry (maid) and Dandy the Dog (1905).

# The Great War

In August 1914, war broke out in Europe. 'Everyone is away!' wailed one socialite, as though the hostilities were a mistimed dinner party. Many upper-class Britons abruptly curtailed their Continental travels; the well-connected Mrs Greville, her great friend Mrs Alice Keppel, and the daughter of Prime Minister Asquith were holidaying together in Holland. Any one of them should have been better informed.

## Patriotism

Patriotic demonstrations ranged from cutting down saplings ceremonially planted a few years before by 'Cousin Willie', the now-vilified Kaiser, to exercising one's dachshunds after dark, so vitriolic was anti-German sentiment. Men of all classes enrolled to fight in Europe; *The Times* exhorted servants to exchange their lives in service for life in the Services. In January 1915, despite a death toll already at 100,000, *Country Life* asked:

*1) Have you a Butler, Groom, Chauffeur, Gardener or Gamekeeper serving you who, at this moment should be serving your King and Country?*

*2) Have you a man serving at your table who should be serving a gun?*

*3) Have you a man digging your garden who should be digging trenches?*

*4) Have you a man driving your car who should be driving a transport wagon?*

*5) Have you a man preserving your game who should be helping to preserve your Country?*

*A great responsibility rests on you. Will you sacrifice your personal convenience for your Country's need? Ask your men to enlist TO-DAY.*

The upper classes encouraged their staff to enrol, even if that necessitated 'mothballing' parts of their houses. Usually, men enlisting were assured that their jobs would be retained for them until their return. At Speke Hall in Liverpool, William Bailey the chauffeur signed up in August 1914; the Armstrong-Siddeley he drove was waiting for him at the end of the war. Thomas Whatmore, a 35-year old valet in 1915, joined the King's Shropshire Light Infantry. He was finally demobilised in March 1919, and in 1920 he became the butler.

Many members of landed families enrolled as officers in their local regiments, often taking their menservants and estate workers with them. Death did not observe rank or high birth; it was the first war in which officers and other ranks, masters and servants, died together so indiscriminately, and on such a vast, almost industrial scale.

## Rationing and staff shortages

At home, while civilians were blissfully ignorant of conditions on the battlefields, some railed against personnel shortages. Lady Sackville complained that she could not run Knole without the full complement of servants. Her old friend Lord Kitchener, the Chief of the Defence Staff, was entreated: 'Do you not realise, my dear Lord K., that we employ five carpenters, and four painters and two blacksmiths and two footmen, and you are taking them all from us!' She concluded, 'I *never* thought I would see parlour maids at Knole!'

## After the War

At the Armistice in November 1918, the reality was devastating. At least 10 million men had been killed. Britain and the Empire lost 947,000 troops. Approximately 1,750,000 British men were wounded, physically and psychologically maimed. When peace returned, the upper classes were desperate to re-instate those who

Below: Soldiers recuperating at Basildon Park near Reading during the First World War.

Above: *Portrait of Adrian Drewe in Uniform*. The photograph is situated in Adrian Drewe's Room at Castle Drogo in Devon. He was killed while on active service in 1917, aged 26.

had been absent for four long years. But attitudes had hardened; many demobilised former servants refused to return to a life of automatic deference and discretion. Men who had fought together in terrible conditions had bonds that breached class boundaries. Lady Londonderry of Mount Stewart complained that girls employed on war work had become ungovernable, demanding double their wages to return to domestic service.

## Economies

The increase in servants' wages and the income tax imposed to fund the war effort greatly increased the cost of staffing grand households. As an economy, Lord Curzon's footmen wore trousers to serve at smaller dinner parties, with knee breeches only worn at dinners of fourteen or more. By contrast, Lady Randolph Churchill recruited 'footmaids', young women in 'livery jackets, striped waistcoats, stiff shirts, short blue skirts, black silk stockings and high-heeled black patent leather shoes'. Invitations to dine *chez* Churchill were highly prized.

## Revolution for women

For working women, the 'call to arms' was revolutionary. The number of female munitions workers increased from 200,000 to 900,000 by 1918. Now, it was not only possible but commendable to be a bus conductress, to run a soldiers' canteen at Waterloo, or to train as a nurse. Patriotism and self-respect were new sensations; the work was hard, but there was an *esprit de corps* that domestic service lacked. Living in their own communities gave women free time with their social equals, far from stuffy housekeepers or butlers. The cities offered exciting pastimes, such as music halls, cinemas and dance halls. Consequently, between 1914 and 1918, about a quarter of the domestic female workforce left service, never to return.

## Changing times

Servants who remained at their posts negotiated higher salaries and better conditions. Nellie Edwards went to work as head housemaid at Sudbury Hall in Derbyshire in 1919, having advertised in a newspaper; she had received 300 letters and 10 telegrams in reply. Competition to secure domestic staff was fierce; senior servants even trawled department stores, looking amongst the customers for respectable widows who needed residential domestic employment.

For many grand houses, the war years were catastrophic. Successive death duties took their toll on depleted family fortunes. Castles and mansions, with their vast estates, now barely staffed and inadequately maintained, were dumped on the property market. For all but the very rich, country-house life was changed forever. Between 1918 and 1921, some 7 million acres (approximately 25 per cent of the acreage of England) were sold.

Middle-class mistresses discovered for the first time how ill-designed their kitchens were, how poorly lit, how cold and damp. However, there were all sorts of 'electric servants' to aid the modern household. With a new vacuum cleaner, a modern oven, and the services of a 'daily' for the worst domestic chores, some householders discovered that there were compensations to life without residential servants, such as greater privacy.

## The death of domestic service?

The most labour-intensive luxurious homes had always relied on a cheap and willing domestic workforce, but the war was the final catalyst. People who previously would have entered service now had other options. Contemporary commentators recognised the sea change, and some lampooned the 'Lady Claras' of the 1920s for their indignation at the lower orders' resistance to working long hours in poor conditions for little pay.

*For myself, I welcome the death of domestic service. There is no reason why it should have been a degrading profession, but society… made it so… not only [has] a social revolution has taken place, but it was long overdue.*

Beverley Nichols, *Sweet and Twenties*, 1958

Paradoxically, the 'treasures' of former eras – the stalwart cook, the taciturn butler and the much-loved nanny – were now more appreciated. For the first time, there was a premium on specialised domestic labour. But for many individuals there were also more important ties of custom and shared heritage. Among the hundreds of thousands of men returning from war, there were those who retained their affection and respect for the 'Big House', and a sense of camaraderie with the people living and working there.

187

# Acknowledgements

Many people assisted and advised the author in researching and writing about this fascinating subject. She would especially like to thank the following individuals who were so generous with their time and expertise:

Carolyn Aldridge
Jacq Barber
Angela Barrett
Joan Bayliss
Sue Baxter
Grant Berry
Chris Blackburn
Emily Blanshard
Jan Brookes
Mike Calnan
Amy Carney
Lissa Chapman
Jeremy Cragg
Alison Dalby
Paul Dearn
Lisa Downes
Harvey Edgington

Sarah Evans
Michelle Fullard
Oliver Garnett
Esther Godfrey
Margaret Gray
Susannah Handley
Siân Harrington
Paul Hawkins
Judith Herbert
Paul Holden
Rachel Hunt
Jonathan Ingram
Patrick Joel
David Kitt
Jim Lee
Helen Lloyd
Helen Long

Sue Lovett
Andrew Loukes
Denise Melhuish
Olive and John Mercer
Paul Meredith
Alexandra Morgan
Simon Osborne
Tina Persaud
Lucy Porten
Kristy Richardson
Christopher Rowell
Teresa Squires
John Stachiewicz
Nino Strachey
Lauren Taylor
Alison Thornhill
Tracie Tungate

Philip Warner
Catrin Wager
Emily Watts
Tom Whatmore
Tessa Wild
Victoria Witty

# Picture credits

Pages 6, 7, 16, 21, 27, 36, 44, 65, 69, 86, 119, 141 © NTPL; Page 106 © NTPL/Michael Caldwell; Page 117, 129 © NTPL/Charlie Waite; Page 143 © NTPL/Derrick E. Witty; Page 4, 9, 29, 43, 48, 56, 62, 82, 93, 103, 113, 135, 136, 142, 148, 153, 155, 159, 161, 162, 185, 186 © NTPL/John Hammond; Page 12, 24, 29, 38, 41, 42, 46, 52, 63, 64, 67, 75, 79, 81, 83, 85, 94, 96, 98, 100, 126, 132, 151, 175, 176 © NTPL/Andreas von Einsiedel; Page 70, 114 © NTPL/Geoff Morgan; Page 2, 22, 23, 40, 45, 51, 58, 84, 89, 101, 104, 115, 121, 166 © NTPL/Nadia Mackenzie; Page 139 © NTPL/Patrick Prendergast; Page 68, 173 © NTPL/Andrew Butler; Page 182 © A.Vesey/NTPL; Page 14, 72, 91, 110 © NTPL/Dennis Gilbert; Page 54, 105 © NTPL/Robert Morris; Page 131 © NTPL/David Levenson; Page 90, 144 © NTPL/John Miller; Page 178 © NTPL/Paul Harris.

Pages 10, 32, 33, 35, 57, 61, 70, 74, 107, 125, 146, 149, 156, 163, 164, 165, 168, 169 © Mary Evans Picture Library; Pages 53, 108, 167, 171 © Mary Evans / The National Archives, London, England; Page 112 © Mary Evans Picture Library / Gill Stoker; Page 132 © Mary Evans Picture Library / Grosvenor Prints; Page 138 © Country Life / IPC Media Ltd / Mary Evans; Page 181 © Mary Evans Picture Library / Onslow Auctions Ltd.

Page 19 © courtesy of the Kevis Collection, West Sussex Record Office.

Page 77 © Private Collection/ Photo © The Maas Gallery, London/ The Bridgeman Art Library.

# Bibliography

**Anon:** *Enquire Within Upon Everything.* First published by Houlston and Sons of Paternoster Square in 1890; this facsimile edition published by Old House Books, 2003

**Anon:** *The Servants' Magazine, or Female Domestics' Instructor*, Volume XIX. Published by Houlston and Stoneman, London, 1856

**Ashenburg, Katherine:** *Clean: An Unsanitised History of Washing.* Published by Profile Books, 2007

**Aslet, Clive and Powers, Alan:** *National Trust Book of the English House.* Published by Penguin Books in association with the National Trust, 1986

**Aslet, Clive:** *The English House; The Story of a Nation at Home.* Published by Bloomsbury, 2008

**Bailey, John:** *Tales from Country Estates.* Published by David & Charles, 1999

**Benson, E.F.:** *The Freaks of Mayfair.* First published in 1916; reprinted by Prion Books, 2003

**Bentley, Nicholas:** *Edwardian Album.* Published by Cardinal, 1974

**Bradford, Sarah:** *Sacheverell Sitwell: Splendours and Miseries.* Published by Sinclair-Stevenson, 1993

**Brears, Peter:** *Penrhyn Servants' Quarters.* Published by the National Trust, 2001

**Cannadine, David:** *The Pleasures of the Past.* This edition published by Penguin Books, 1997

**Davies, Jennifer:** *The Victorian Kitchen.* Published by BBC Books, 1989

**De Courcy, Anne:** *The Viceroy's Daughters: The Lives of the Curzon Sisters.* Published in paperback by Phoenix, 2001

**Delafield, E.M.:** *Diary of a Provincial Lady*, first published 1930. This edition published by Virago, 2000

**Dillon, Maureen:** *Artificial Sunshine: A Social History of Domestic Lighting.* Published by the National Trust, 2002

**Durant, David N.:** *Life in the Country House: A Historical Dictionary.* Published by John Murray, 1996

**Flanders, Judith:** *The Victorian House: Domestic Life from Childbirth to Deathbed.* Published by HarperCollins, 2003

**Garnett, Oliver:** *Country House Pastimes.* Published by the National Trust, 1998

**Garnett, Oliver and Owen, Diana:** *Petworth: A Souvenir Guide.* Published by the National Trust, 2006

**Gibbons, Ed:** *All Beer and Skittles? A Short History of Inns and Taverns.* Published by the National Trust, 2001

**Girouard, Mark:** *Hardwick Hall.* First published 1989 by the National Trust; this edition reprinted 2000

**Girouard, Mark:** *Life in the English Country House.* Published by Yale University Press, 1978

**Girouard, Mark:** *The Victorian Country House.* Published by Yale University Press; this edition published 1985

**Gorst, Frederick:** *Of Carriages and Kings.* Published by Allen Lane, 1956

**Grossmith, G. and W.:** *The Diary of a Nobody*, 1892; reprinted London, 1983

**Hardyment, Christina:** *Behind the Scenes; Domestic Arrangements in Historic Houses.* This edition published by the National Trust, 1997

**Holroyd, Michael:** *Bernard Shaw.* Published by Vintage, 1998

**Horn, Pamela:** *The Rise and Fall of the Victorian Servant.* Sutton Publishing, this edition published 2004

**Hughes, Kathryn:** *The Victorian Governess.* Published by Hambledon Press, 1993

**Hughes, Kathryn:** *The Short Life and Long Times of Mrs Beeton.* Published by Fourth Estate, 2005

**Jenkins, Simon:** *England's Thousand Best Houses.* This edition published by Penguin Books, 2009

**Jennings, Charles:** *Them and Us: The American Invasion of British High Society.* Published by Sutton Publishing, 2007

**Keppel, Sonia:** *Edwardian Daughter.* Published by Hamish Hamilton, 1958

**Kerr, Robert:** *The Gentleman's House, or How to Plan English Residences.* Published by John Murray, 1864

**Laurie, Kedrun:** *Cricketer Preferred: Estate Workers at Lyme Park*, 1898–1946. Published by the Lyme Park Joint Committee, 1980

**Light, Alison:** *Mrs Woolf and the Servants.* Published by Penguin Books, 2008

**Little, May:** *A Year's Dinners: 365 Seasonable Dinners with Instructions for Cooking.* Published by Harrods Ltd, 1930

**Long, Helen:** *The Edwardian House.* Published by Manchester University Press, 1993

**Maddison, John:** *Felbrigg Hall.* First published 1995 by the National Trust; this edition reprinted 2000

**Marsh, Jan:** *William Morris and Red House.* Published by National Trust Books, 2005

**Matthews, R. Borlase:** *Electricity for Everyone.* Published by The Electrical Press, 1909

**May, Trevor:** *The Victorian Domestic Servant.* Published by Shire Library, 2009

**Miller, James:** *Fertile Fortune: The Story of Tyntesfield.* Published by National Trust Books, 2006

**Musson, Jeremy:** *Up and Down Stairs: The History of the Country House Servant.* Published by John Murray, 2009

**Nichols, Beverley:** *Down the Kitchen Sink: a Memoir.* This edition published by Timber Press, USA, 2006

**Nichols, Beverley:** *Sweet and Twenties.* Published by Weidenfeld & Nicolson, 1958

**Nichols, Beverley:** *All I Could Never Be.* Published by Jonathan Cape, 1949

**Nicolson, Juliet:** *The Great Silence: 1918–1920 Living in the Shadow of the Great War.* Published by John Murray, 2010

**Owen, Diana:** *Petworth: The Servants' Quarters.* Published by the National Trust, 1997

**Palmer, Arnold:** *Moveable Feasts.* Published by Oxford University Press, 1984

## Bibliography continued:

**Pearson, John:** *Stags and Serpents: The Story of the House of Cavendish and the Dukes of Devonshire*. Published by Macmillan London Ltd, 1983

**Phillips, R. Randal:** 'The Servantless House'. Published by *Country Life* and George Newnes Ltd, London, 1920

**Post, Emily:** *Etiquette*. First published by Funk and Wagnall of New York, 1922

**Rothwell, James:** *Dunham Massey*. Published by the National Trust, 2000

**Rowell, Christopher:** *Uppark*. Published by the National Trust; this edition published 1999

**Sackville-West, Vita:** *Knole and the Sackvilles*. First published 1922; this edition republished 1991 by the National Trust

**Sackville-West, Vita:** *The Edwardians*. Tenth impression, published by The Hogarth Press, 1930

**Sambrook, Pamela:** *A Country House at Work: Three Centuries of Dunham Massey*. Published by the National Trust, 2003

**Sambrook, Pamela:** *Keeping Their Place: Domestic Service in the Country House*. Published by Sutton Publishing Limited, 2005

**Sandeman, Phyllis Elinor:** *Treasures on Earth*. Published by the Lyme Park Joint Committee, 1981

**Sitwell, Osbert:** *Laughter in the Next Room*. This edition published by the Reprint Society, 1950

**Smith, Susanna:** *The Workhouse, Southwell*. Published by the National Trust, 2002

**Stevenson, J.J.:** *House Architecture* (Vol. II). Published by Macmillan and Co., London, 1880 (Fellow of the Royal Institute of British Architects)

**Strong, Sir Roy:** *Country Life 1897–1997: The English Arcadia*. Published by Country Life Books and Boxtree Ltd, 1996

**Sykes, Christopher Simon:** *The Big House: The Story of a Country House and its Family*. This edition published by Harper Perennial, 2005

**Tobin, Shelley:** *Inside Out: A Brief History of Underwear*. Published by the National Trust, 2000

**Turner, E.S.:** *What the Butler Saw: Two Hundred and Fifty years of the Servant Problem*. Published by Michael Joseph, 1962

**Various:** *The National Trust Manual of Housekeeping*. Published by Butterworth-Heinemann, 2006

**Visser, Margaret:** *The Rituals of Dinner: The Origins, Evolution, Eccentricities and Meaning of Table Manners*. Published by Viking, 1992

**Waugh, Evelyn:** *Brideshead Revisited*, first published by Chapman & Hall 1945; this edition reprinted in Penguin Classics, 2000

**Weaver, Rebecca and Dale, Rodney:** *Machines in the Home*. Published by the British Library, 1992

**Whatmore, Tom:** *My Life at Speke Hall*. Published by Countyvise Ltd, 2009

**Wilson, A.N.:** *The Victorians*. Published by Hutchinson, 2002

**Wodehouse, P.G.:** *Life at Blandings: Something Fresh, Summer Lightning and Heavy Weather*. Published as a compilation by Penguin Books, 1979

**Wyndham, Ursula:** *Astride the Wall: A Memoir 1913–1945*. Published by Lennard Publishing, 1988

# Index